Amazon Athena User Guide

A catalogue record for this book is available from the Hong Kong Public Libraries.

Published in Hong Kong by Samurai Media Limited.

Email: info@samuraimedia.org

ISBN 9789888408870

Contents

What is Amazon Athena?

Amazon Athena is an interactive query service that makes it easy to analyze data directly in Amazon Simple Storage Service (Amazon S3) using standard SQL. With a few actions in the AWS Management Console, you can point Athena at your data stored in Amazon S3 and begin using standard SQL to run ad-hoc queries and get results in seconds.

Athena is serverless, so there is no infrastructure to set up or manage, and you pay only for the queries you run. Athena scales automatically—executing queries in parallel—so results are fast, even with large datasets and complex queries.

When should I use Athena?

Athena helps you analyze unstructured, semi-structured, and structured data stored in Amazon S3. Examples include CSV, JSON, or columnar data formats such as Apache Parquet and Apache ORC. You can use Athena to run ad-hoc queries using ANSI SQL, without the need to aggregate or load the data into Athena.

Athena integrates with the AWS Glue Data Catalog, which offers a persistent metadata store for your data in Amazon S3. This allows you to create tables and query data in Athena based on a central metadata store available throughout your AWS account and integrated with the ETL and data discovery features of AWS Glue. For more information, see Integration with AWS Glue and What is AWS Glue in the *AWS Glue Developer Guide*.

Athena integrates with Amazon QuickSight for easy data visualization.

You can use Athena to generate reports or to explore data with business intelligence tools or SQL clients connected with a JDBC or an ODBC driver. For more information, see What is Amazon QuickSight in the *Amazon QuickSight User Guide* and Connecting to Amazon Athena with ODBC and JDBC Drivers.

You can create named queries with AWS CloudFormation and run them in Athena. Named queries allow you to map a query name to a query and then call the query multiple times referencing it by its name. For information, see CreateNamedQuery in the *Amazon Athena API Reference*, and AWS::Athena::NamedQuery in the *AWS CloudFormation User Guide*.

Accessing Athena

You can access Athena using the AWS Management Console, through a JDBC connection, using the Athena API, or using the Athena CLI.

- To get started with the console, see Getting Started.
- To learn how to use JDBC, see Connecting to Amazon Athena with JDBC.
- To use the Athena API, see the Amazon Athena API Reference.
- To use the CLI, install the AWS CLI and then type `aws athena help` from the command line to see available commands. For information about available commands, see the AWS Athena command line reference.

Understanding Tables, Databases, and the Data Catalog

In Athena, tables and databases are containers for the metadata definitions that define a schema for underlying source data. For each dataset, a table needs to exist in Athena. The metadata in the table tells Athena where the data is located in Amazon S3, and specifies the structure of the data, for example, column names, data types, and the name of the table. Databases are a logical grouping of tables, and also hold only metadata and schema information for a dataset.

For each dataset that you'd like to query, Athena must have an underlying table it will use for obtaining and returning query results. Therefore, before querying data, a table must be registered in Athena. The registration occurs when you either create tables automatically or manually.

Regardless of how the tables are created, the tables creation process registers the dataset with Athena. This registration occurs either in the AWS Glue Data Catalog, or in the internal Athena data catalog and enables Athena to run queries on the data.

- To create a table automatically, use an AWS Glue crawler from within Athena. For more information about AWS Glue and crawlers, see Integration with AWS Glue. When AWS Glue creates a table, it registers it in its own AWS Glue Data Catalog. Athena uses the AWS Glue Data Catalog to store and retrieve this metadata, using it when you run queries to analyze the underlying dataset.

The AWS Glue Data Catalog is accessible throughout your AWS account. Other AWS services can share the AWS Glue Data Catalog, so you can see databases and tables created throughout your organization using Athena and vice versa. In addition, AWS Glue lets you automatically discover data schema and extract, transform, and load (ETL) data.

Note
You use the internal Athena data catalog in regions where AWS Glue is not available and where the AWS Glue Data Catalog cannot be used.

- To create a table manually:
  - Use the Athena console to run the **Create Table Wizard**.
  - Use the Athena console to write Hive DDL statements in the Query Editor.
  - Use the Athena API or CLI to execute a SQL query string with DDL statements.
  - Use the Athena JDBC or ODBC driver.

When you create tables and databases manually, Athena uses HiveQL data definition language (DDL) statements such as `CREATE TABLE`, `CREATE DATABASE`, and `DROP TABLE` under the hood to create tables and databases in the AWS Glue Data Catalog, or in its internal data catalog in those regions where AWS Glue is not available.

Note
If you have tables in Athena created before August 14, 2017, they were created in an Athena-managed data catalog that exists side-by-side with the AWS Glue Data Catalog until you choose to update. For more information, see Upgrading to the AWS Glue Data Catalog Step-by-Step.

When you query an existing table, under the hood, Amazon Athena uses Presto, a distributed SQL engine. We have examples with sample data within Athena to show you how to create a table and then issue a query against it using Athena. Athena also has a tutorial in the console that helps you get started creating a table based on data that is stored in Amazon S3.

- For a step-by-step tutorial on creating a table and write queries in the Athena Query Editor, see Getting Started.
- Run the Athena tutorial in the console. This launches automatically if you log in to https://console.aws.amazon.com/athena/ for the first time. You can also choose **Tutorial** in the console to launch it.

Release Notes

Describes Amazon Athena features, improvements, and bug fixes by release date.

Contents

June 5, 2018

Published on *2018-06-05*

Topics

- Support for Views
- Improvements and Updates to Error Messages
- Bug Fixes

Support for Views

Added support for views. You can now use CREATE VIEW, DESCRIBE VIEW, DROP VIEW, SHOW CREATE VIEW, and SHOW VIEWS in Athena. The query that defines the view runs each time you reference the view in your query. For more information, see Views.

Improvements and Updates to Error Messages

- Included a GSON 2.8.0 library into the CloudTrail SerDe, to solve an issue with the CloudTrail SerDe and enable parsing of JSON strings.
- Enhanced partition schema validation in Athena for Parquet, and, in some cases, for ORC, by allowing reordering of columns. This enables Athena to better deal with changes in schema evolution over time, and with tables added by the AWS Glue Crawler. For more information, see Handling Schema Updates.
- Added parsing support for `SHOW VIEWS`.
- Made the following improvements to most common error messages:
  - Replaced an Internal Error message with a descriptive error message when a SerDe fails to parse the column in an Athena query. Previously, Athena issued an internal error in cases of parsing errors. The new error message reads: "HIVE_BAD_DATA: Error parsing field value for field 0: java.lang.String cannot be cast to org.openx.data.jsonserde.json.JSONObject".
  - Improved error messages about insufficient permissions by adding more detail.

Bug Fixes

Fixed the following bugs:

- Fixed an issue that enables the internal translation of `REAL` to `FLOAT` data types. This improves integration with the AWS Glue Crawler that returns `FLOAT` data types.
- Fixed an issue where Athena was not converting AVRO `DECIMAL` (a logical type) to a `DECIMAL` type.
- Fixed an issue where Athena did not return results for queries on Parquet data with `WHERE` clauses that referenced values in the `TIMESTAMP` data type.

May 17, 2018

Published on *2018-05-17*

Increased query concurrency limits in Athena from five to twenty. This means that you can submit and run up to twenty DDL queries and twenty SELECT queries at a time. Note that the concurrency limits are separate for DDL and SELECT queries.

Concurrency limits in Athena are defined as the number of queries that can be submitted to the service concurrently. You can submit up to twenty queries of the same type (DDL or SELECT) at a time. If you submit a query that exceeds the concurrent query limit, the Athena API displays an error message: "You have exceeded the limit for the number of queries you can run concurrently. Reduce the number of concurrent queries submitted by this account. Contact customer support to request a concurrent query limit increase."

After you submit your queries to Athena, it processes the queries by assigning resources based on the overall service load and the amount of incoming requests. We continuously monitor and make adjustments to the service so that your queries process as fast as possible.

For information, see Service Limits. This is a soft limit and you can request a limit increase for concurrent queries.

April 19, 2018

Published on *2018-04-19*

Released the new version of the JDBC driver (version 2.0.2) with support for returning the `ResultSet` data as an Array data type, improvements, and bug fixes. For details, see the Release Notes for the driver.

For information about downloading the new JDBC driver version 2.0.2 and its documentation, see Using Athena with the JDBC Driver.

The latest version of the JDBC driver is 2.0.2. If you are migrating from a 1.x driver to a 2.x driver, you will need to migrate your existing configurations to the new configuration. We highly recommend that you migrate to the current driver.

For information about the changes introduced in the new version of the driver, the version differences, and examples, see the JDBC Driver Migration Guide.

For information about the previous version of the JDBC driver, see Using Athena with the Previous Version of the JDBC Driver.

April 6, 2018

Published on *2018-04-06*

Use auto-complete to type queries in the Athena console.

March 15, 2018

Published on *2018-03-15*

Added an ability to automatically create Athena tables for CloudTrail log files directly from the CloudTrail console. For information, see Creating a Table for CloudTrail Logs in the CloudTrail Console.

February 2, 2018

Published on *2018-02-12*

Added an ability to securely offload intermediate data to disk for memory-intensive queries that use the `GROUP BY` clause. This improves the reliability of such queries, preventing "Query resource exhausted" errors.

January 19, 2018

Published on *2018-01-19*

Athena uses Presto, an open-source distributed query engine, to run queries.

With Athena, there are no versions to manage. We have transparently upgraded the underlying engine in Athena to a version based on Presto version 0.172. No action is required on your end.

With the upgrade, you can now use Presto 0.172 Functions and Operators, including Presto 0.172 Lambda Expressions in Athena.

Major updates for this release, including the community-contributed fixes, include:

- Support for ignoring headers. You can use the `skip.header.line.count` property when defining tables, to allow Athena to ignore headers. This is currently supported for queries that use the OpenCSV SerDe, and not for Grok or Regex SerDes.
- Support for the `CHAR(n)` data type in `STRING` functions. The range for `CHAR(n)` is `[1.255]`, while the range for `VARCHAR(n)` is `[1,65535]`.
- Support for correlated subqueries.
- Support for Presto Lambda expressions and functions.
- Improved performance of the `DECIMAL` type and operators.
- Support for filtered aggregations, such as `SELECT sum(col_name)FILTER`, where `id > 0`.
- Push-down predicates for the `DECIMAL`, `TINYINT`, `SMALLINT`, and `REAL` data types.
- Support for quantified comparison predicates: `ALL`, `ANY`, and `SOME`.
- Added functions: https://prestodb.io/docs/0.172/functions/array.html#arrays_overlap, https://prestodb.io/docs/0.172/functions/array.html#array_except, https://prestodb.io/docs/0.172/functions/string.html#levenshtein_distance, https://prestodb.io/docs/0.172/functions/string.html#codepoint, https://prestodb.io/docs/0.172/functions/aggregate.html#skewness, https://prestodb.io/docs/0.172/functions/aggregate.html#kurtosis, and https://prestodb.io/docs/0.172/functions/conversion.html#typeof.
- Added a variant of the https://prestodb.io/docs/0.172/functions/datetime.html#from_unixtime function that takes a timezone argument.
- Added the https://prestodb.io/docs/0.172/functions/aggregate.html#bitwise_and_agg and https://prestodb.io/docs/0.172/functions/aggregate.html#bitwise_or_agg aggregation functions.
- Added the https://prestodb.io/docs/0.172/functions/binary.html#xxhash64 and https://prestodb.io/docs/0.172/functions/binary.html#to_big_endian_64 functions.
- Added support for escaping double quotes or backslashes using a backslash with a JSON path subscript to the https://prestodb.io/docs/0.172/functions/json.html#json_extract and https://prestodb.io/docs/0.172/functions/json.html#json_extract_scalar functions. This changes the semantics of any invocation using a backslash, as backslashes were previously treated as normal characters.

For a complete list of functions and operators, see SQL Queries, Functions, and Operators in this guide, and Presto 0.172 Functions.

Athena does not support all of Presto's features. For more information, see Limitations.

November 13, 2017

Published on *2017-11-13*

Added support for connecting Athena to the ODBC Driver. For information, see Connecting to Amazon Athena with ODBC.

November 1, 2017

Published on *2017-11-01*

Added support for querying geospatial data, and for Asia Pacific (Seoul), Asia Pacific (Mumbai), and EU (London) regions. For information, see Querying Geospatial Data and AWS Regions and Endpoints.

October 19, 2017

Published on *2017-10-19*

Added support for EU (Frankfurt). For a list of supported regions, see AWS Regions and Endpoints.

October 3, 2017

Published on *2017-10-03*

Create named Athena queries with CloudFormation. For more information, see AWS::Athena::NamedQuery in the *AWS CloudFormation User Guide*.

September 25, 2017

Published on *2017-09-25*

Added support for Asia Pacific (Sydney). For a list of supported regions, see AWS Regions and Endpoints.

August 14, 2017

Published on *2017-08-14*

Added integration with the AWS Glue Data Catalog and a migration wizard for updating from the Athena managed data catalog to the AWS Glue Data Catalog. For more information, see Integration with AWS Glue.

August 4, 2017

Published on *2017-08-04*

Added support for Grok SerDe, which provides easier pattern matching for records in unstructured text files such as logs. For more information, see Grok SerDe. Added keyboard shortcuts to scroll through query history using the console (CTRL + / using Windows, CMD + / using Mac).

June 22, 2017

Published on *2017-06-22*

Added support for Asia Pacific (Tokyo) and Asia Pacific (Singapore). For a list of supported regions, see AWS Regions and Endpoints.

June 8, 2017

Published on *2017-06-08*

Added support for EU (Ireland). For more information, see AWS Regions and Endpoints.

May 19, 2017

Published on *2017-05-19*

Added an Amazon Athena API and AWS CLI support for Athena; updated JDBC driver to version 1.1.0; fixed various issues.

- Amazon Athena enables application programming for Athena. For more information, see Amazon Athena API Reference. The latest AWS SDKs include support for the Athena API. For links to documentation and downloads, see the *SDKs* section in Tools for Amazon Web Services.
- The AWS CLI includes new commands for Athena. For more information, see the AWS CLI Reference for Athena.
- A new JDBC driver 1.1.0 is available, which supports the new Athena API as well as the latest features and bug fixes. Download the driver at https://s3.amazonaws.com/athena-downloads/drivers/AthenaJDBC41-1.1.0.jar. We recommend upgrading to the latest Athena JDBC driver; however, you may still use the earlier driver version. Earlier driver versions do not support the Athena API. For more information, see Using Athena with the JDBC Driver.
- Actions specific to policy statements in earlier versions of Athena have been deprecated. If you upgrade to JDBC driver version 1.1.0 and have customer-managed or inline IAM policies attached to JDBC users, you must update the IAM policies. In contrast, earlier versions of the JDBC driver do not support the Athena API, so you can specify only deprecated actions in policies attached to earlier version JDBC users. For this reason, you shouldn't need to update customer-managed or inline IAM policies.
- These policy-specific actions were used in Athena before the release of the Athena API. Use these deprecated actions in policies **only** with JDBC drivers earlier than version 1.1.0. If you are upgrading the JDBC driver, replace policy statements that allow or deny deprecated actions with the appropriate API actions as listed or errors will occur:

Deprecated Policy-Specific Action	Corresponding Athena API Action
athena:RunQuery	athena:StartQueryExecution
athena:CancelQueryExecution	athena:StopQueryExecution
athena:GetQueryExecutions	athena:ListQueryExecutions

Improvements

- Increased the query string length limit to 256 KB.

Bug Fixes

- Fixed an issue that caused query results to look malformed when scrolling through results in the console.
- Fixed an issue where a \u0000 character string in Amazon S3 data files would cause errors.
- Fixed an issue that caused requests to cancel a query made through the JDBC driver to fail.
- Fixed an issue that caused the AWS CloudTrail SerDe to fail with Amazon S3 data in US East (Ohio).
- Fixed an issue that caused DROP TABLE to fail on a partitioned table.

April 4, 2017

Published on *2017-04-04*

Added support for Amazon S3 data encryption and released JDBC driver update (version 1.0.1) with encryption support, improvements, and bug fixes.

Features

- Added the following encryption features:
  - Support for querying encrypted data in Amazon S3.
  - Support for encrypting Athena query results.
- A new version of the driver supports new encryption features, adds improvements, and fixes issues.
- Added the ability to add, replace, and change columns using **ALTER TABLE**. For more information, see Alter Column in the Hive documentation.
- Added support for querying LZO-compressed data.

For more information, see Configuring Encryption Options.

Improvements

- Better JDBC query performance with page-size improvements, returning 1,000 rows instead of 100.
- Added ability to cancel a query using the JDBC driver interface.
- Added ability to specify JDBC options in the JDBC connection URL. For more information, see Using Athena with the Previous Version of the JDBC Driver for the previous version of the driver, and Connect with the JDBC, for the most current version.
- Added PROXY setting in the driver, which can now be set using ClientConfiguration in the AWS SDK for Java.

Bug Fixes

Fixed the following bugs:

- Throttling errors would occur when multiple queries were issued using the JDBC driver interface.
- The JDBC driver would abort when projecting a decimal data type.
- The JDBC driver would return every data type as a string, regardless of how the data type was defined in the table. For example, selecting a column defined as an **INT** data type using **resultSet.GetObject()** would return a **STRING** data type instead of **INT**.
- The JDBC driver would verify credentials at the time a connection was made, rather than at the time a query would run.
- Queries made through the JDBC driver would fail when a schema was specified along with the URL.

March 24, 2017

Published on *2017-03-24*

Added the AWS CloudTrail SerDe, improved performance, fixed partition issues.

Features

- Added the AWS CloudTrail SerDe. For more information, see CloudTrail SerDe. For detailed usage examples, see the AWS Big Data Blog post, Analyze Security, Compliance, and Operational Activity Using AWS CloudTrail and Amazon Athena.

Improvements

- Improved performance when scanning a large number of partitions.
- Improved performance on `MSCK Repair Table` operation.
- Added ability to query Amazon S3 data stored in regions other than your primary region. Standard inter-region data transfer rates for Amazon S3 apply in addition to standard Athena charges.

Bug Fixes

- Fixed a bug where a "table not found error" might occur if no partitions are loaded.
- Fixed a bug to avoid throwing an exception with `ALTER TABLE ADD PARTITION IF NOT EXISTS` queries.
- Fixed a bug in `DROP PARTITIONS`.

February 20, 2017

Published on *2017-02-20*

Added support for AvroSerDe and OpenCSVSerDe, US East (Ohio) region, and bulk editing columns in the console wizard. Improved performance on large Parquet tables.

Features

- **Introduced support for new SerDes:**
  - Avro SerDe
  - OpenCSVSerDe for Processing CSV

- **US East (Ohio)** region (**us-east-2**) launch. You can now run queries in this region.

- You can now use the **Add Table** wizard to define table schema in bulk. Choose **Catalog Manager**, **Add table**, and then choose **Bulk add columns** as you walk through the steps to define the table.

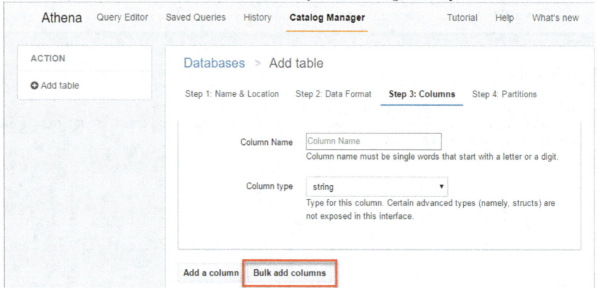

Type name value pairs in the text box and choose **Add**.

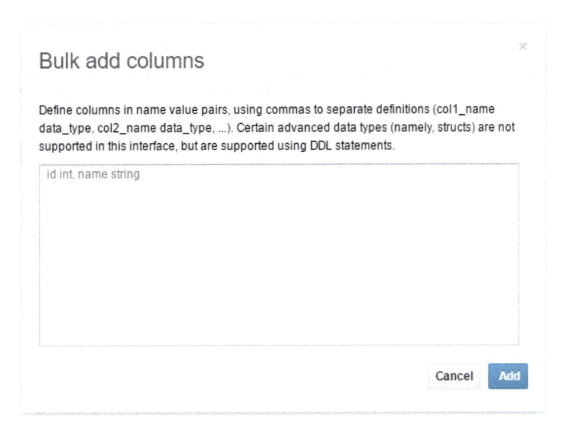

Bulk add columns

Define columns in name value pairs, using commas to separate definitions (col1_name
data_type, col2_name data_type, ...). Certain advanced data types (namely, structs) are not
supported in this interface, but are supported using DDL statements.

id int, name string

Cancel   Add

Improvements

- Improved performance on large Parquet tables.

Setting Up

If you've already signed up for Amazon Web Services (AWS), you can start using Amazon Athena immediately. If you haven't signed up for AWS, or if you need assistance querying data using Athena, first complete the tasks below:

Sign Up for AWS

When you sign up for AWS, your account is automatically signed up for all services in AWS, including Athena. You are charged only for the services that you use. When you use Athena, you use Amazon S3 to store your data. Athena has no AWS Free Tier pricing.

If you have an AWS account already, skip to the next task. If you don't have an AWS account, use the following procedure to create one.

To create an AWS account

1. Open http://aws.amazon.com/, and then choose **Create an AWS Account**.
2. Follow the online instructions. Part of the sign-up procedure involves receiving a phone call and entering a PIN using the phone keypad.

Note your AWS account number, because you need it for the next task.

Create an IAM User

An AWS Identity and Access Management (IAM) user is an account that you create to access services. It is a different user than your main AWS account. As a security best practice, we recommend that you use the IAM user's credentials to access AWS services. Create an IAM user, and then add the user to an IAM group with administrative permissions or and grant this user administrative permissions. You can then access AWS using a special URL and the credentials for the IAM user.

If you signed up for AWS but have not created an IAM user for yourself, you can create one using the IAM console. If you aren't familiar with using the console, see Working with the AWS Management Console.

To create a group for administrators

1. Sign in to the IAM console at https://console.aws.amazon.com/iam/.
2. In the navigation pane, choose **Groups**, **Create New Group**.
3. For **Group Name**, type a name for your group, such as `Administrators`, and choose **Next Step**.
4. In the list of policies, select the check box next to the **AdministratorAccess** policy. You can use the **Filter** menu and the **Search** field to filter the list of policies.
5. Choose **Next Step**, **Create Group**. Your new group is listed under **Group Name**.

To create an IAM user for yourself, add the user to the administrators group, and create a password for the user

1. In the navigation pane, choose **Users**, and then **Create New Users**.
2. For **1**, type a user name.

3. Clear the check box next to **Generate an access key for each user** and then **Create**.

4. In the list of users, select the name (not the check box) of the user you just created. You can use the **Search** field to search for the user name.

5. Choose **Groups, Add User to Groups**.

6. Select the check box next to the administrators and choose **Add to Groups**.

7. Choose the **Security Credentials** tab. Under **Sign-In Credentials**, choose **Manage Password**.

8. Choose **Assign a custom password**. Then type a password in the **Password** and **Confirm Password** fields. When you are finished, choose **Apply**.

9. To sign in as this new IAM user, sign out of the AWS console, then use the following URL, where `your_aws_account_id` is your AWS account number without the hyphens (for example, if your AWS account number is 1234-5678-9012, your AWS account ID is 123456789012):

```
1  https://*your_account_alias*.signin.aws.amazon.com/console/
```

It is also possible the sign-in link will use your account name instead of number. To verify the sign-in link for IAM users for your account, open the IAM console and check under **IAM users sign-in link** on the dashboard.

Attach Managed Policies for Using Athena

Attach Athena managed policies to the IAM account you use to access Athena. There are two managed policies for Athena: `AmazonAthenaFullAccess` and `AWSQuicksightAthenaAccess`. These policies grant permissions to Athena to query Amazon S3 as well as write the results of your queries to a separate bucket on your behalf. For more information and step-by-step instructions, see Attaching Managed Policies in the *AWS Identity and Access Management User Guide*. For information about policy contents, see IAM Policies for User Access.

Note

You may need additional permissions to access the underlying dataset in Amazon S3. If you are not the account owner or otherwise have restricted access to a bucket, contact the bucket owner to grant access using a resource-based bucket policy, or contact your account administrator to grant access using an identity-based policy. For more information, see Amazon S3 Permissions. If the dataset or Athena query results are encrypted, you may need additional permissions. For more information, see Configuring Encryption Options.

Getting Started

This tutorial walks you through using Amazon Athena to query data. You'll create a table based on sample data stored in Amazon Simple Storage Service, query the table, and check the results of the query.

The tutorial is using live resources, so you are charged for the queries that you run. You aren't charged for the sample datasets that you use, but if you upload your own data files to Amazon S3, charges do apply.

Prerequisites

If you have not already done so, sign up for an account in Setting Up.

Step 1: Create a Database

You first need to create a database in Athena.

To create a database

1. Open the Athena console.

2. If this is your first time visiting the Athena console, you'll go to a Getting Started page. Choose **Get Started** to open the Query Editor. If it isn't your first time, the Athena Query Editor opens.

3. In the Athena Query Editor, you see a query pane with an example query. Start typing your query anywhere in the query pane.

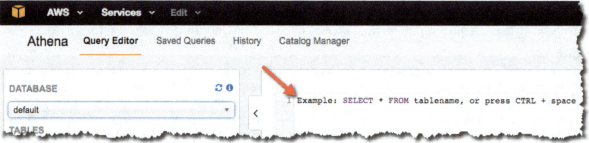

4. To create a database named `mydatabase`, enter the following CREATE DATABASE statement, and then choose **Run Query**:

```
1 CREATE DATABASE mydatabase
```

5. Confirm that the catalog display refreshes and `mydatabase` appears in the **DATABASE** list in the **Catalog** dashboard on the left side.

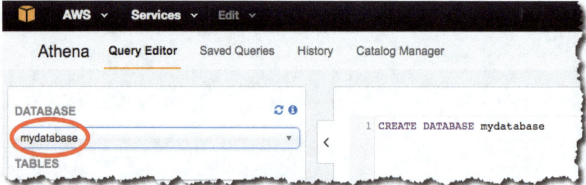

Step 2: Create a Table

Now that you have a database, you're ready to create a table that's based on the sample data file. You define columns that map to the data, specify how the data is delimited, and provide the location in Amazon S3 for the file.

To create a table

1. Make sure that `mydatabase` is selected for **DATABASE** and then choose **New Query**.

2. In the query pane, enter the following CREATE TABLE statement, and then choose **Run Query**: Note You can query data in regions other than the region where you run Athena. Standard inter-region data transfer rates for Amazon S3 apply in addition to standard Athena charges. To reduce data transfer charges, replace *myregion* in **s3://athena-examples-myregion/path/to/data/** with the region identifier where you run Athena, for example, **s3://athena-examples-us-east-1/path/to/data/**.

```
1  CREATE EXTERNAL TABLE IF NOT EXISTS cloudfront_logs (
2    `Date` DATE,
3    Time STRING,
4    Location STRING,
5    Bytes INT,
6    RequestIP STRING,
7    Method STRING,
8    Host STRING,
9    Uri STRING,
10   Status INT,
11   Referrer STRING,
12   os STRING,
13   Browser STRING,
14   BrowserVersion STRING
15   ) ROW FORMAT SERDE 'org.apache.hadoop.hive.serde2.RegexSerDe'
16   WITH SERDEPROPERTIES (
17   "input.regex" = "^(?!#)([^ ]+)\\s+([^ ]+)\\s+([^ ]+)\\s+([^ ]+)\\s+([^ ]+)\\s+([^ ]+)\\s
        +([^ ]+)\\s+([^ ]+)\\s+([^ ]+)\\s+([^ ]+)\\s+[^\(]+[\(]([^\;]+).*\%20([^\/]+)[\/](.*)
        $"
18   ) LOCATION 's3://athena-examples-myregion/cloudfront/plaintext/';
```

The `table cloudfront_logs` is created and appears in the **Catalog** dashboard for your database.

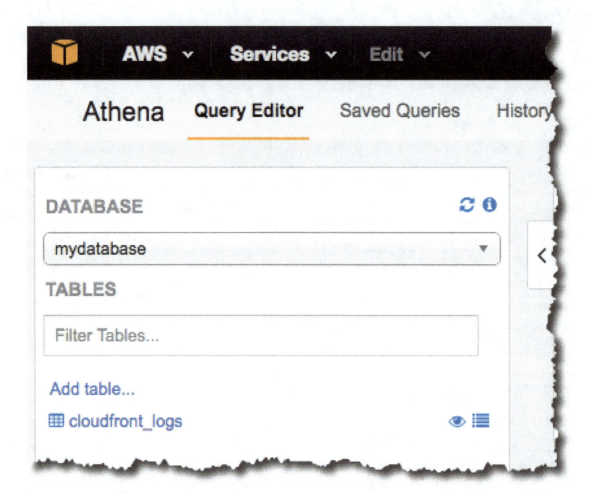

Step 3: Query Data

Now that you have the `cloudfront_logs` table created in Athena based on the data in Amazon S3, you can run queries on the table and see the results in Athena.

To run a query

1. Choose **New Query**, enter the following statement anywhere in the query pane, and then choose **Run Query**:

```
1 SELECT os, COUNT(*) count
2 FROM cloudfront_logs
3 WHERE date BETWEEN date '2014-07-05' AND date '2014-08-05'
4 GROUP BY os;
```

   Results are returned that look like the following:

	os	count
1	iOS	794
2	MacOS	852
3	OSX	799
4	Windows	883
5	Linux	813
6	Android	855

2. Optionally, you can save the results of a query to CSV by choosing the file icon on the **Results** pane.

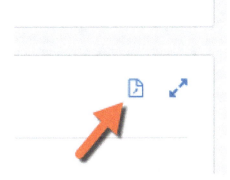

You can also view the results of previous queries or queries that may take some time to complete. Choose **History** then either search for your query or choose **View** or **Download** to view or download the results of previous completed queries. This also displays the status of queries that are currently running. Query history is retained for 45 days. For information, see Viewing Query History.

Query results are also stored in Amazon S3 in a bucket called aws-athena-query-results-*ACCOUNTID-REGION*. You can change the default location in the console and encryption options by choosing **Settings** in the upper right pane. For more information, see Query Results.

Accessing Amazon Athena

You can access Amazon Athena using the AWS Management Console, the Amazon Athena API, or the AWS CLI.

Using the Console

You can use the AWS Management Console for Amazon Athena to do the following:

- Create or select a database.
- Create, view, and delete tables.
- Filter tables by starting to type their names.
- Preview tables and generate CREATE TABLE DDL for them.
- Show table properties.
- Run queries on tables, save and format queries, and view query history.
- Create up to ten queries using different query tabs in the query editor. To open a new tab, click the plus sign.
- Display query results, save, and export them.
- Access the AWS Glue Data Catalog.
- View and change settings, such as view the query result location, configure auto-complete, and encrypt query results.

In the right pane, the Query Editor displays an introductory screen that prompts you to create your first table. You can view your tables under **Tables** in the left pane.

Here's a high-level overview of the actions available for each table:

- **Preview tables** – View the query syntax in the Query Editor on the right.
- **Show properties** – Show a table's name, its location in Amazon S3, input and output formats, the serialization (SerDe) library used, and whether the table has encrypted data.
- **Delete table** – Delete a table.
- **Generate CREATE TABLE DDL** – Generate the query behind a table and view it in the query editor.

Using the API

Amazon Athena enables application programming for Athena. For more information, see Amazon Athena API Reference. The latest AWS SDKs include support for the Athena API.

For examples of using the AWS SDK for Java with Athena, see Code Samples.

For more information about AWS SDK documentation and downloads, see the *SDKs* section in Tools for Amazon Web Services.

Using the CLI

You can access Amazon Athena using the AWS CLI. For more information, see the AWS CLI Reference for Athena.

Integration with AWS Glue

AWS Glue is a fully managed ETL (extract, transform, and load) service that can categorize your data, clean it, enrich it, and move it reliably between various data stores. AWS Glue crawlers automatically infer database and table schema from your source data, storing the associated metadata in the AWS Glue Data Catalog. When you create a table in Athena, you can choose to create it using an AWS Glue crawler.

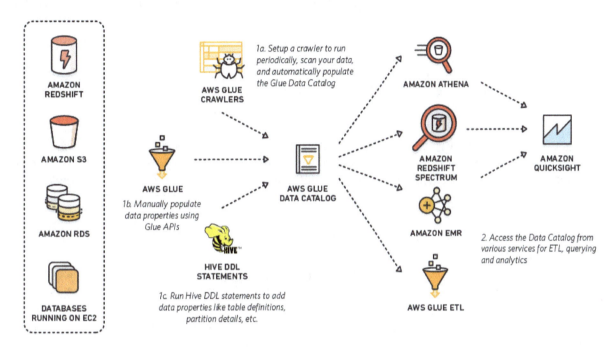

In regions where AWS Glue is supported, Athena uses the AWS Glue Data Catalog as a central location to store and retrieve table metadata throughout an AWS account. The Athena execution engine requires table metadata that instructs it where to read data, how to read it, and other information necessary to process the data. The AWS Glue Data Catalog provides a unified metadata repository across a variety of data sources and data formats, integrating not only with Athena, but with Amazon S3, Amazon RDS, Amazon Redshift, Amazon Redshift Spectrum, Amazon EMR, and any application compatible with the Apache Hive metastore.

For more information about the AWS Glue Data Catalog, see Populating the AWS Glue Data Catalog in the *AWS Glue Developer Guide*. For a list of regions where AWS Glue is available, see Regions and Endpoints in the *AWS General Reference*.

Separate charges apply to AWS Glue. For more information, see AWS Glue Pricing and Are there separate charges for AWS Glue? For more information about the benefits of using AWS Glue with Athena, see Why should I upgrade to the AWS Glue Data Catalog?

Topics

- Upgrading to the AWS Glue Data Catalog Step-by-Step
- FAQ: Upgrading to the AWS Glue Data Catalog
- Best Practices When Using Athena with AWS Glue

Upgrading to the AWS Glue Data Catalog Step-by-Step

Amazon Athena manages its own data catalog until the time that AWS Glue releases in the Athena region. At that time, if you previously created databases and tables using Athena or Amazon Redshift Spectrum, you can choose to upgrade Athena to the AWS Glue Data Catalog. If you are new to Athena, you don't need to make any changes; databases and tables are available to Athena using the AWS Glue Data Catalog and vice versa. For more information about the benefits of using the AWS Glue Data Catalog, see FAQ: Upgrading to the AWS Glue Data Catalog. For a list of regions where AWS Glue is available, see Regions and Endpoints in the *AWS General Reference*.

Until you upgrade, the Athena-managed data catalog continues to store your table and database metadata, and you see the option to upgrade at the top of the console. The metadata in the Athena-managed catalog isn't available in the AWS Glue Data Catalog or vice versa. While the catalogs exist side-by-side, you aren't able to create tables or databases with the same names, and the creation process in either AWS Glue or Athena fails in this case.

We created a wizard in the Athena console to walk you through the steps of upgrading to the AWS Glue console. The upgrade takes just a few minutes, and you can pick up where you left off. For more information about each upgrade step, see the topics in this section. For more information about working with data and tables in the AWS Glue Data Catalog, see the guidelines in Best Practices When Using Athena with AWS Glue.

Step 1 - Allow a User to Perform the Upgrade

By default, the action that allows a user to perform the upgrade is not allowed in any policy, including any managed policies. Because the AWS Glue Data Catalog is shared throughout an account, this extra failsafe prevents someone from accidentally migrating the catalog.

Before the upgrade can be performed, you need to attach a customer-managed IAM policy, with a policy statement that allows the upgrade action, to the user who performs the migration.

The following is an example policy statement.

```
1  {
2      "Version": "2012-10-17",
3      "Statement": [
4          {
5              "Effect": "Allow",
6              "Action": [
7                  "glue:ImportCatalogToGlue "
8              ],
9              "Resource": [ "*" ]
10         }
11     ]
12 }
```

Step 2 - Update Customer-Managed/Inline Policies Associated with Athena Users

If you have customer-managed or inline IAM policies associated with Athena users, you need to update the policy or policies to allow actions that AWS Glue requires. If you use the managed policy, they are automatically updated. The AWS Glue policy actions to allow are listed in the example policy below. For the full policy statement, see IAM Policies for User Access.

```
1  {
2    "Effect":"Allow",
3    "Action":[
```

```
 4      "glue:CreateDatabase",
 5      "glue:DeleteDatabase",
 6      "glue:GetDatabase",
 7      "glue:GetDatabases",
 8      "glue:UpdateDatabase",
 9      "glue:CreateTable",
10      "glue:DeleteTable",
11      "glue:BatchDeleteTable",
12      "glue:UpdateTable",
13      "glue:GetTable",
14      "glue:GetTables",
15      "glue:BatchCreatePartition",
16      "glue:CreatePartition",
17      "glue:DeletePartition",
18      "glue:BatchDeletePartition",
19      "glue:UpdatePartition",
20      "glue:GetPartition",
21      "glue:GetPartitions",
22      "glue:BatchGetPartition"
23    ],
24    "Resource":[
25      "*"
26    ]
27 }
```

Step 3 - Choose Upgrade in the Athena Console

After you make the required IAM policy updates, choose **Upgrade** in the Athena console. Athena moves your metadata to the AWS Glue Data Catalog. The upgrade takes only a few minutes. After you upgrade, the Athena console has a link to open the AWS Glue Catalog Manager from within Athena.

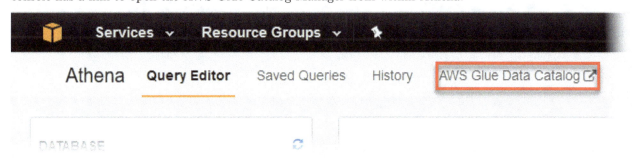

When you create a table using the console, you now have the option to create a table using an AWS Glue crawler. For more information, see Using AWS Glue Crawlers.

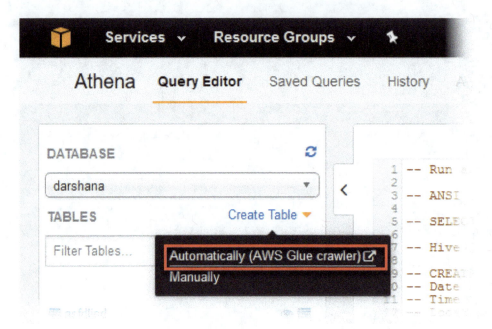

FAQ: Upgrading to the AWS Glue Data Catalog

If you created databases and tables using Athena in a region before AWS Glue was available in that region, metadata is stored in an Athena-managed data catalog, which only Athena and Amazon Redshift Spectrum can access. To use AWS Glue features together with Athena and Redshift Spectrum, you must upgrade to the AWS Glue Data Catalog. Athena can only be used together with the AWS Glue Data Catalog in regions where AWS Glue is available. For a list of regions, see Regions and Endpoints in the *AWS General Reference.*

Why should I upgrade to the AWS Glue Data Catalog?

AWS Glue is a completely-managed extract, transform, and load (ETL) service. It has three main components:

- **An AWS Glue crawler** can automatically scan your data sources, identify data formats, and infer schema.
- **A fully managed ETL service** allows you to transform and move data to various destinations.
- **The AWS Glue Data Catalog** stores metadata information about databases and tables, pointing to a data store in Amazon S3 or a JDBC-compliant data store.

For more information, see AWS Glue Concepts.

Upgrading to the AWS Glue Data Catalog has the following benefits.

Unified metadata repository

The AWS Glue Data Catalog provides a unified metadata repository across a variety of data sources and data formats. It provides out-of-the-box integration with Amazon Simple Storage Service (Amazon S3), Amazon Relational Database Service (Amazon RDS), Amazon Redshift, Amazon Redshift Spectrum, Athena, Amazon EMR, and any application compatible with the Apache Hive metastore. You can create your table definitions one time and query across engines.

For more information, see Populating the AWS Glue Data Catalog.

Automatic schema and partition recognition

AWS Glue crawlers automatically crawl your data sources, identify data formats, and suggest schema and transformations. Crawlers can help automate table creation and automatic loading of partitions that you can query using Athena, Amazon EMR, and Redshift Spectrum. You can also create tables and partitions directly using the AWS Glue API, SDKs, and the AWS CLI.

For more information, see Cataloging Tables with a Crawler.

Easy-to-build pipelines

The AWS Glue ETL engine generates Python code that is entirely customizable, reusable, and portable. You can edit the code using your favorite IDE or notebook and share it with others using GitHub. After your ETL job is ready, you can schedule it to run on the fully managed, scale-out Spark infrastructure of AWS Glue. AWS Glue handles provisioning, configuration, and scaling of the resources required to run your ETL jobs, allowing you to tightly integrate ETL with your workflow.

For more information, see Authoring AWS Glue Jobs in the *AWS Glue Developer Guide.*

Are there separate charges for AWS Glue?

Yes. With AWS Glue, you pay a monthly rate for storing and accessing the metadata stored in the AWS Glue Data Catalog, an hourly rate billed per second for AWS Glue ETL jobs and crawler runtime, and an hourly rate billed per second for each provisioned development endpoint. The AWS Glue Data Catalog allows you to store up to a million objects at no charge. If you store more than a million objects, you are charged USD$1 for each 100,000 objects over a million. An object in the AWS Glue Data Catalog is a table, a partition, or a database. For more information, see AWS Glue Pricing.

Upgrade process FAQ

- Who can perform the upgrade?
- My users use a managed policy with Athena and Redshift Spectrum. What steps do I need to take to upgrade?
- What happens if I don't upgrade?
- Why do I need to add AWS Glue policies to Athena users?
- What happens if I don't allow AWS Glue policies for Athena users?
- Is there risk of data loss during the upgrade?
- Is my data also moved during this upgrade?

Who can perform the upgrade?

You need to attach a customer-managed IAM policy with a policy statement that allows the upgrade action to the user who will perform the migration. This extra check prevents someone from accidentally migrating the catalog for the entire account. For more information, see Step 1 - Allow a User to Perform the Upgrade.

My users use a managed policy with Athena and Redshift Spectrum. What steps do I need to take to upgrade?

The Athena managed policy has been automatically updated with new policy actions that allow Athena users to access AWS Glue. However, you still must explicitly allow the upgrade action for the user who performs the upgrade. To prevent accidental upgrade, the managed policy does not allow this action.

What happens if I don't upgrade?

If you don't upgrade, you are not able to use AWS Glue features together with the databases and tables you create in Athena or vice versa. You can use these services independently. During this time, Athena and AWS Glue both prevent you from creating databases and tables that have the same names in the other data catalog. This prevents name collisions when you do upgrade.

Why do I need to add AWS Glue policies to Athena users?

Before you upgrade, Athena manages the data catalog, so Athena actions must be allowed for your users to perform queries. After you upgrade to the AWS Glue Data Catalog, Athena actions no longer apply to accessing the AWS Glue Data Catalog, so AWS Glue actions must be allowed for your users. Remember, the managed policy for Athena has already been updated to allow the required AWS Glue actions, so no action is required if you use the managed policy.

What happens if I don't allow AWS Glue policies for Athena users?

If you upgrade to the AWS Glue Data Catalog and don't update a user's customer-managed or inline IAM policies, Athena queries fail because the user won't be allowed to perform actions in AWS Glue. For the specific actions to allow, see Step 2 - Update Customer-Managed/Inline Policies Associated with Athena Users.

Is there risk of data loss during the upgrade?

No.

Is my data also moved during this upgrade?

No. The migration only affects metadata.

Best Practices When Using Athena with AWS Glue

When using Athena with the AWS Glue Data Catalog, you can use AWS Glue to create databases and tables (schema) to be queried in Athena, or you can use Athena to create schema and then use them in AWS Glue and related services. This topic provides considerations and best practices when using either method.

Under the hood, Athena uses Presto to execute DML statements and Hive to execute the DDL statements that create and modify schema. With these technologies, there are a couple conventions to follow so that Athena and AWS Glue work well together.

In this topic

- Database, Table, and Column Names
-

** Using AWS Glue Crawlers **

- Scheduling a Crawler to Keep the AWS Glue Data Catalog and Amazon S3 in Sync
- Using Multiple Data Sources with Crawlers
- Syncing Partition Schema to Avoid "HIVE_PARTITION_SCHEMA_MISMATCH"
- Updating Table Metadata
-

** Working with CSV Files **

- CSV Data Enclosed in Quotes
- CSV Files with Headers
-

** Using AWS Glue Jobs for ETL with Athena **

- Creating Tables Using Athena for AWS Glue ETL Jobs
- Using ETL Jobs to Optimize Query Performance
- Converting SMALLINT and TINYINT Datatypes to INT When Converting to ORC
- Changing Date Data Types to String for Parquet ETL Transformation
- Automating AWS Glue Jobs for ETL

Database, Table, and Column Names

When you create schema in AWS Glue to query in Athena, consider the following:

- A database name cannot be longer than 252 characters.
- A table name cannot be longer than 255 characters.
- A column name cannot be longer than 128 characters.
- The only acceptable characters for database names, table names, and column names are lowercase letters, numbers, and the underscore character.

You can use the AWS Glue Catalog Manager to rename columns, but at this time table names and database names cannot be changed using the AWS Glue console. To correct database names, you need to create a new database and copy tables to it (in other words, copy the metadata to a new entity). You can follow a similar process for tables. You can use the AWS Glue SDK or AWS CLI to do this.

Using AWS Glue Crawlers

AWS Glue crawlers help discover and register the schema for datasets in the AWS Glue Data Catalog. The crawlers go through your data, and inspect portions of it to determine the schema. In addition, the crawler can detect and register partitions. For more information, see Cataloging Data with a Crawler in the *AWS Glue Developer Guide*.

Scheduling a Crawler to Keep the AWS Glue Data Catalog and Amazon S3 in Sync

AWS Glue crawlers can be set up to run on a schedule or on demand. For more information, see Time-Based Schedules for Jobs and Crawlers in the *AWS Glue Developer Guide*.

If you have data that arrives for a partitioned table at a fixed time, you can set up an AWS Glue crawler to run on schedule to detect and update table partitions. This can eliminate the need to run a potentially long and expensive `MSCK REPAIR` command or manually execute an `ALTER TABLE ADD PARTITION` command. For more information, see Table Partitions in the *AWS Glue Developer Guide*.

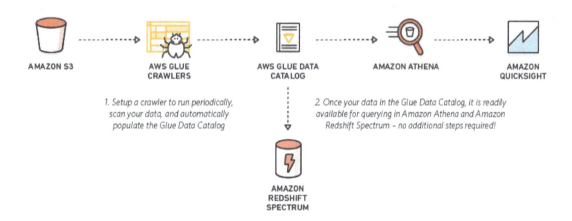

Using Multiple Data Sources with Crawlers

When an AWS Glue crawler scans Amazon S3 and detects multiple directories, it uses a heuristic to determine where the root for a table is in the directory structure, and which directories are partitions for the table. In some cases, where the schema detected in two or more directories is similar, the crawler may treat them as partitions instead of separate tables. One way to help the crawler discover individual tables is to add each table's root directory as a data store for the crawler.

The following partitions in Amazon S3 are an example:

```
1 s3://bucket01/folder1/table1/partition1/file.txt
2 s3://bucket01/folder1/table1/partition2/file.txt
3 s3://bucket01/folder1/table1/partition3/file.txt
4 s3://bucket01/folder1/table2/partition4/file.txt
5 s3://bucket01/folder1/table2/partition5/file.txt
```

If the schema for `table1` and `table2` are similar, and a single data source is set to `s3://bucket01/folder1/` in AWS Glue, the crawler may create a single table with two partition columns: one partition column that contains `table1` and `table2`, and a second partition column that contains `partition1` through `partition5`.

To have the AWS Glue crawler create two separate tables as intended, use the AWS Glue console to set the crawler to have two data sources, `s3://bucket01/folder1/table1/` and `s3://bucket01/folder1/table2`, as shown in the following procedure.

To add another data store to an existing crawler in AWS Glue

1. In the AWS Glue console, choose **Crawlers**, select your crawler, and then choose **Action**, **Edit crawler**.

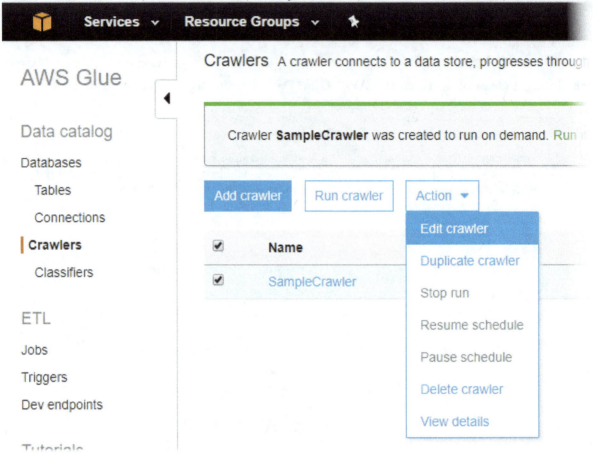

2. Under **Add information about your crawler**, choose additional settings as appropriate, and then choose **Next**.

3. Under **Add a data store**, change **Include path** to the table-level directory. For instance, given the example above, you would change it from s3://bucket01/folder1 to s3://bucket01/folder1/table1/. Choose **Next**.

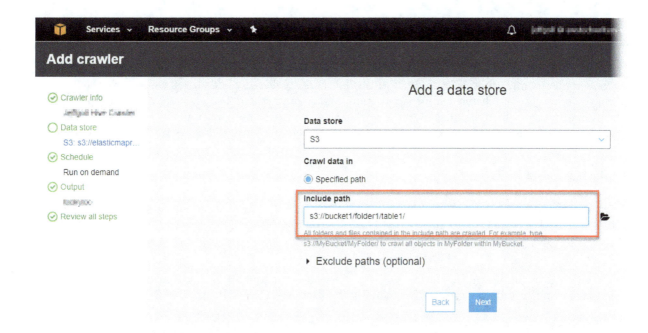

4. For **Add another data store**, choose **Yes**, **Next**.

5. For **Include path**, enter your other table-level directory (for example, s3://bucket01/folder1/table2/) and choose **Next**.

   1. Repeat steps 3-5 for any additional table-level directories, and finish the crawler configuration.

The new values for **Include locations** appear under data stores

Syncing Partition Schema to Avoid "HIVE_PARTITION_SCHEMA_MISMATCH"

For each table within the AWS Glue Data Catalog that has partition columns, the schema is stored at the table level and for each individual partition within the table. The schema for partitions are populated by an AWS Glue crawler based on the sample of data that it reads within the partition. For more information, see Using Multiple Data Sources with Crawlers.

When Athena runs a query, it validates the schema of the table and the schema of any partitions necessary for the query. The validation compares the column data types in order and makes sure that they match for the columns that overlap. This prevents unexpected operations such as adding or removing columns from the middle of a table. If Athena detects that the schema of a partition differs from the schema of the table, Athena may not be able to process the query and fails with `HIVE_PARTITION_SCHEMA_MISMATCH`.

There are a few ways to fix this issue. First, if the data was accidentally added, you can remove the data files that cause the difference in schema, drop the partition, and re-crawl the data. Second, you can drop the individual partition and then run `MSCK REPAIR` within Athena to re-create the partition using the table's schema. This second option works only if you are confident that the schema applied will continue to read the data correctly.

Updating Table Metadata

After a crawl, the AWS Glue crawler automatically assigns certain table metadata to help make it compatible with other external technologies like Apache Hive, Presto, and Spark. Occasionally, the crawler may incorrectly assign metadata properties. Manually correct the properties in AWS Glue before querying the table using Athena. For more information, see Viewing and Editing Table Details in the *AWS Glue Developer Guide*.

AWS Glue may mis-assign metadata when a CSV file has quotes around each data field, getting the `serializationLib` property wrong. For more information, see CSV Data Enclosed in quotes.

Working with CSV Files

CSV files occasionally have quotes around the data values intended for each column, and there may be header values included in CSV files, which aren't part of the data to be analyzed. When you use AWS Glue to create schema from these files, follow the guidance in this section.

CSV Data Enclosed in Quotes

If you run a query in Athena against a table created from a CSV file with quoted data values, update the table definition in AWS Glue so that it specifies the right SerDe and SerDe properties. This allows the table definition to use the OpenCSVSerDe. For more information about the OpenCSV SerDe, see OpenCSVSerDe for Processing CSV.

In this case, make the following changes:

- Change the `serializationLib` property under field in the `SerDeInfo` field in the table to `org.apache.hadoop.hive.serde2.OpenCSVSerde`.
- Enter appropriate values for `separatorChar`, `quoteChar`, and `escapeChar`. The `separatorChar` value is a comma, the `quoteChar` value is double quotes ("), and the `escapeChar` value is the backslash (\).

For example, for a CSV file with records such as the following:

```
1  "John","Doe","123-555-1231","John said \"hello\""
2  "Jane","Doe","123-555-9876","Jane said \"hello\""
```

You can use the AWS Glue console to edit table details as shown in this example:

Edit table details

Table name

sample_csv_table

Input format

org.apache.hadoop.mapred.TextInputFormat

Output format

org.apache.hadoop.hive.ql.io.HiveIgnoreKeyTextOutputFormat

Serde name

Serde serialization lib

org.apache.hadoop.hive.serde2.OpenCSVSerde

Serde parameters

Key	Value	
escapeChar	\	✖
quoteChar	"	✖
separatorChar	,	✖
Type key...	Type value...	

Description

Apply

Alternatively, you can update the table definition in AWS Glue to have a SerDeInfo block such as the following:

```
1  "SerDeInfo": {
2      "name": "",
```

```
3    "serializationLib": "org.apache.hadoop.hive.serde2.OpenCSVSerde",
4    "parameters": {
5        "separatorChar": ",",
6        "quoteChar": """,
7        "escapeChar": "\\"
8        }
9 },
```

For more information, see Viewing and Editing Table Details in the *AWS Glue Developer Guide*.

CSV Files with Headers

If you are writing CSV files from AWS Glue to query using Athena, you must remove the CSV headers so that the header information is not included in Athena query results. One way to achieve this is to use AWS Glue jobs, which perform extract, transform, and load (ETL) work. You can write scripts in AWS Glue using a language that is an extension of the PySpark Python dialect. For more information, see Authoring Jobs in Glue in the *AWS Glue Developer Guide*.

The following example shows a function in an AWS Glue script that writes out a dynamic frame using `from_options`, and sets the `writeHeader` format option to false, which removes the header information:

```
1 glueContext.write_dynamic_frame.from_options(frame = applymapping1, connection_type = "s3",
      connection_options = {"path": "s3://MYBUCKET/MYTABLEDATA/"}, format = "csv", format_options
      = {"writeHeader": False}, transformation_ctx = "datasink2")
```

Using AWS Glue Jobs for ETL with Athena

AWS Glue jobs perform ETL operations. An AWS Glue job runs a script that extracts data from sources, transforms the data, and loads it into targets. For more information, see Authoring Jobs in Glue in the *AWS Glue Developer Guide*.

Creating Tables Using Athena for AWS Glue ETL Jobs

Tables that you create from within Athena must have a table property added to them called a `classification`, which identifies the format of the data. This allows AWS Glue to be able to use the tables for ETL jobs. The classification values can be `csv`, `parquet`, `orc`, `avro`, or `json`. An example create table statement in Athena follows:

```
1 CREATE EXTERNAL TABLE sampleTable (
2    column1 INT,
3    column2 INT
4    ) STORED AS PARQUET
5    TBLPROPERTIES (
6    'classification'='parquet')
```

If the table property was not added when the table was created, the property can be added using the AWS Glue console.

To change the classification property using the console

1.

Choose Edit Table.

1.

For Classification, select the file type and choose Apply.

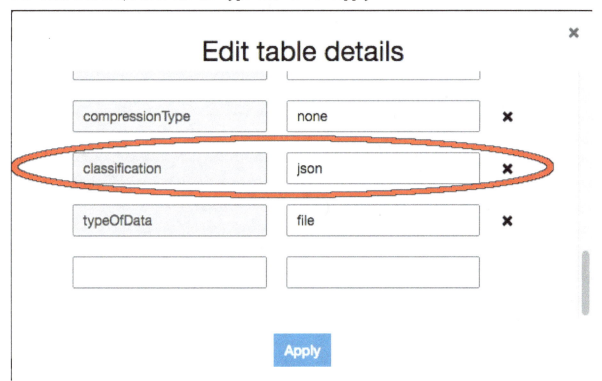

For more information, see Working with Tables in the *AWS Glue Developer Guide*.

Using ETL Jobs to Optimize Query Performance

AWS Glue jobs can help you transform data to a format that optimizes query performance in Athena. Data formats have a large impact on query performance and query costs in Athena.

We recommend the Parquet and ORC formats. AWS Glue supports writing to both of these data formats, which can make it easier and faster for you to transform data to an optimal format for Athena. For more information about these formats and other ways to improve performance, see Top Performance Tuning tips for Amazon Athena.

Converting SMALLINT and TINYINT Datatypes to INT When Converting to ORC

To reduce the likelihood that Athena is unable to read the `SMALLINT` and `TINYINT` data types produced by an AWS Glue ETL job, convert `SMALLINT` and `TINYINT` to `INT` when using the wizard or writing a script for an ETL job.

Changing Date Data Types to String for Parquet ETL Transformation

Athena currently does not support the `DATE` data type for Parquet files. Convert `DATE` data types to `STRING` when using the wizard or writing a script for an AWS Glue ETL job.

Automating AWS Glue Jobs for ETL

You can configure AWS Glue ETL jobs to run automatically based on triggers. This feature is ideal when data from outside AWS is being pushed to an S3 bucket in a suboptimal format for querying in Athena. For more information, see Triggering AWS Glue Jobs in the *AWS Glue Developer Guide*.

Connecting to Amazon Athena with ODBC and JDBC Drivers

To explore and visualize your data with business intelligence tools, download, install, and configure an ODBC (Open Database Connectivity) or JDBC (Java Database Connectivity) driver.

Topics

- Using Athena with the JDBC Driver
- Connecting to Amazon Athena with ODBC

Using Athena with the JDBC Driver

You can use a JDBC connection to connect Athena to business intelligence tools, such as SQL Workbench. To do this, download, install, and configure the Athena JDBC driver, using the following link on Amazon S3.

Migration from Previous Version of the JDBC Driver

The current JDBC driver version 2.x is *not* a drop-in replacement of the previous version of the JDBC driver, and is *not* backwards compatible with the JDBC driver version 1.x that you used before.

Important
The latest version of the JDBC driver is 2.0.2. If you are migrating from a 1.x driver to a 2.x driver, you will need to migrate your existing configurations to the new configuration. We highly recommend that you migrate to the current driver.
For information about the changes introduced in the new version of the driver, the version differences, and examples, see the JDBC Driver Migration Guide.
For information about the previous version of the JDBC driver, see Using Athena with the Previous Version of the JDBC Driver.

Links for Downloading the JDBC Driver

The JDBC driver complies with the JDBC API 4.1 and 4.2 data standards.

Note
The JDBC driver version 2.x is not available for JDK 6.0 (Java 1.6), and is not compatible with JDBC API version 4.0.

Before downloading the driver, check which version of Java Runtime Environment (JRE) you use. The JRE version depends on the version of the JDBC API you are using with the driver. If you are not sure, download the latest version of the driver.

Download the driver that matches your version of the JDK and the JDBC data standards.

- The AthenaJDBC41-2.0.2.jar is compatible with JDBC 4.1 and requires JDK 7.0 or later.
- The AthenaJDBC42-2.0.2.jar is compatible with JDBC 4.2 and requires JDK 8.0 or later.

JDBC Driver Release Notes, License Agreement, and Notices

After you download the version you need, read the release notes, and review the License Agreement and Notices.

- Release Notes
- License Agreement
- Notices

Now you are ready to migrate from the previous version and install and configure this version of the JDBC driver.

JDBC Driver Documentation

To install and configure the JDBC driver version 2.x, see the JDBC Driver Installation and Configuration Guide.

To migrate from the previous version of the JDBC driver to this driver, see the JDBC Driver Migration Guide.

Connecting to Amazon Athena with ODBC

Download the ODBC driver, the Amazon Athena ODBC driver License Agreement, and the documentation for the driver using the following links.

Amazon Athena ODBC Driver License Agreement

License Agreement

Windows

- Windows 32 bit ODBC Driver
- Windows 64 bit ODBC Driver

Linux

- Linux 32 bit ODBC Driver
- Linux 64 bit ODBC Driver

OSX

OSX ODBC Driver

ODBC Driver Connection String

For information about the connection string to use with your application, see ODBC Driver Installation and Configuration Guide.

Documentation

ODBC Driver Installation and Configuration Guide.

Security

Amazon Athena uses IAM policies to restrict access to Athena operations. Encryption options enable you to encrypt query result files in Amazon S3 and query data encrypted in Amazon S3. Users must have the appropriate permissions to access the Amazon S3 locations and decrypt files.

Topics

- Setting User and Amazon S3 Bucket Permissions
- Configuring Encryption Options

Setting User and Amazon S3 Bucket Permissions

To run queries in Athena, you must have the appropriate permissions for:

- The Athena actions.
- The Amazon S3 locations where the underlying data is stored that you are going to query in Athena.

If you are an administrator for other users, make sure that they have appropriate permissions associated with their user profiles.

IAM Policies for User Access

To allow or deny Athena service actions for yourself or other users, use IAM policies attached to principals, such as users or groups.

Each IAM policy consists of statements that define the actions that are allowed or denied. For a list of actions, see the Amazon Athena API Reference.

Managed policies are easy to use and are automatically updated with the required actions as the service evolves.

The `AmazonAthenaFullAccess` policy is the managed policy for Athena. Attach this policy to users and other principals who need full access to Athena. For more information and step-by-step instructions for attaching a policy to a user, see Attaching Managed Policies in the *AWS Identity and Access Management User Guide.*

Customer-managed and *inline* policies allow you to specify more granular Athena actions within a policy to fine-tune access. We recommend that you use the `AmazonAthenaFullAccess` policy as a starting point and then allow or deny specific actions listed in the Amazon Athena API Reference. For more information about inline policies, see Managed Policies and Inline Policies in the *AWS Identity and Access Management User Guide.*

If you also have principals that connect using JDBC, you must allow additional actions not listed in the API. For more information, see Service Actions for JDBC Connections.

AmazonAthenaFullAccess Managed Policy

Managed policy contents change, so the policy shown here may be out-of-date. Check the IAM console for the most up-to-date policy.

```
 1  {
 2      "Version": "2012-10-17",
 3      "Statement": [
 4          {
 5              "Effect": "Allow",
 6              "Action": [
 7                  "athena:*"
 8              ],
 9              "Resource": [
10                  "*"
11              ]
12          },
13          {
14              "Effect": "Allow",
15              "Action": [
16                  "glue:CreateDatabase",
17                  "glue:DeleteDatabase",
18                  "glue:GetDatabase",
19                  "glue:GetDatabases",
```

```
20          "glue:UpdateDatabase",
21          "glue:CreateTable",
22          "glue:DeleteTable",
23          "glue:BatchDeleteTable",
24          "glue:UpdateTable",
25          "glue:GetTable",
26          "glue:GetTables",
27          "glue:BatchCreatePartition",
28          "glue:CreatePartition",
29          "glue:DeletePartition",
30          "glue:BatchDeletePartition",
31          "glue:UpdatePartition",
32          "glue:GetPartition",
33          "glue:GetPartitions",
34          "glue:BatchGetPartition"
35        ],
36        "Resource": [
37          "*"
38        ]
39      },
40      {
41        "Effect": "Allow",
42        "Action": [
43          "s3:GetBucketLocation",
44          "s3:GetObject",
45          "s3:ListBucket",
46          "s3:ListBucketMultipartUploads",
47          "s3:ListMultipartUploadParts",
48          "s3:AbortMultipartUpload",
49          "s3:CreateBucket",
50          "s3:PutObject"
51        ],
52        "Resource": [
53          "arn:aws:s3:::aws-athena-query-results-*"
54        ]
55      },
56      {
57        "Effect": "Allow",
58        "Action": [
59          "s3:GetObject"
60        ],
61        "Resource": [
62          "arn:aws:s3:::athena-examples*"
63        ]
64      }
65    ]
66 }
```

AWSQuicksightAthenaAccess Managed Policy

An additional managed policy, `AWSQuicksightAthenaAccess`, grants access to actions that Amazon QuickSight needs to integrate with Athena. This policy includes deprecated actions for Athena that are not in the API. Attach this policy only to principals who use Amazon QuickSight in conjunction with Athena.

Managed policy contents change, so the policy shown here may be out-of-date. Check the IAM console for the most up-to-date policy.

```
1  {
2      "Version": "2012-10-17",
3      "Statement": [
4          {
5              "Effect": "Allow",
6              "Action": [
7                  "athena:BatchGetQueryExecution",
8                  "athena:CancelQueryExecution",
9                  "athena:GetCatalogs",
10                 "athena:GetExecutionEngine",
11                 "athena:GetExecutionEngines",
12                 "athena:GetNamespace",
13                 "athena:GetNamespaces",
14                 "athena:GetQueryExecution",
15                 "athena:GetQueryExecutions",
16                 "athena:GetQueryResults",
17                 "athena:GetTable",
18                 "athena:GetTables",
19                 "athena:ListQueryExecutions",
20                 "athena:RunQuery",
21                 "athena:StartQueryExecution",
22                 "athena:StopQueryExecution"
23             ],
24             "Resource": [
25                 "*"
26             ]
27         },
28         {
29             "Effect": "Allow",
30             "Action": [
31                 "glue:CreateDatabase",
32                 "glue:DeleteDatabase",
33                 "glue:GetDatabase",
34                 "glue:GetDatabases",
35                 "glue:UpdateDatabase",
36                 "glue:CreateTable",
37                 "glue:DeleteTable",
38                 "glue:BatchDeleteTable",
39                 "glue:UpdateTable",
40                 "glue:GetTable",
41                 "glue:GetTables",
42                 "glue:BatchCreatePartition",
43                 "glue:CreatePartition",
44                 "glue:DeletePartition",
45                 "glue:BatchDeletePartition",
46                 "glue:UpdatePartition",
47                 "glue:GetPartition",
48                 "glue:GetPartitions",
49                 "glue:BatchGetPartition"
50             ],
51             "Resource": [
52                 "*"
```

```
53            ]
54        },
55        {
56            "Effect": "Allow",
57            "Action": [
58                "s3:GetBucketLocation",
59                "s3:GetObject",
60                "s3:ListBucket",
61                "s3:ListBucketMultipartUploads",
62                "s3:ListMultipartUploadParts",
63                "s3:AbortMultipartUpload",
64                "s3:CreateBucket",
65                "s3:PutObject"
66            ],
67            "Resource": [
68                "arn:aws:s3:::aws-athena-query-results-*"
69            ]
70        }
71    ]
72 }
```

Access through JDBC Connections

To gain access to AWS services and resources, such as Athena and the Amazon S3 buckets, provide JDBC driver credentials to your application. See Connect with the JDBC Driver.

Amazon S3 Permissions

In addition to the allowed actions for Athena that you define in policies, if you or your users need to create tables and work with underlying data, you must grant appropriate access to the Amazon S3 location of the data.

You can do this using user policies, bucket policies, or both. For detailed information and scenarios about how to grant Amazon S3 access, see Example Walkthroughs: Managing Access in the *Amazon Simple Storage Service Developer Guide*. For more information and an example of which Amazon S3 actions to allow, see the example bucket policy later in this topic.

Note
Athena does not support restricting or allowing access to Amazon S3 resources based on the `aws:SourceIp` condition key.

Cross-account Permissions

A common scenario is granting access to users in an account different from the bucket owner so that they can perform queries. In this case, use a bucket policy to grant access.

The following example bucket policy, created and applied to bucket `s3://my-athena-data-bucket` by the bucket owner, grants access to all users in account `123456789123`, which is a different account.

```
1 {
2    "Version": "2012-10-17",
3    "Id": "MyPolicyID",
4    "Statement": [
5        {
6            "Sid": "MyStatementSid",
```

```
 7          "Effect": "Allow",
 8          "Principal": {
 9              "AWS": "arn:aws:iam::123456789123:root"
10          },
11          "Action": [
12              "s3:GetBucketLocation",
13              "s3:GetObject",
14              "s3:ListBucket",
15              "s3:ListBucketMultipartUploads",
16              "s3:ListMultipartUploadParts",
17              "s3:AbortMultipartUpload",
18              "s3:PutObject"
19          ],
20          "Resource": [
21              "arn:aws:s3:::my-athena-data-bucket",
22              "arn:aws:s3:::my-athena-data-bucket/*"
23          ]
24      }
25    ]
26 }
```

To grant access to a particular user in an account, replace the `Principal` key with a key that specifies the user instead of `root`. For example, for user profile `Dave`, use `arn:aws:iam::123456789123:user/Dave`.

Configuring Encryption Options

You can use Athena to query encrypted data in Amazon S3 by indicating data encryption when you create a table. You can also choose to encrypt the results of all queries in Amazon S3, which Athena stores in a location known as the *S3 staging directory*. You can encrypt query results stored in Amazon S3 whether the underlying dataset is encrypted in Amazon S3 or not. You set up query-result encryption using the Athena console or, if you connect using the JDBC driver, by configuring driver options. You specify the type of encryption to use and the Amazon S3 staging directory location. Query-result encryption applies to all queries.

These options encrypt data at rest in Amazon S3. Regardless of whether you use these options, transport layer security (TLS) encrypts objects in-transit between Athena resources and between Athena and Amazon S3. Query results stream to JDBC clients as plain text and are encrypted using SSL.

Important
The setup for querying an encrypted dataset in Amazon S3 and the options in Athena to encrypt query results are independent. Each option is enabled and configured separately. You can use different encryption methods or keys for each. This means that reading encrypted data in Amazon S3 doesn't automatically encrypt Athena query results in Amazon S3. The opposite is also true. Encrypting Athena query results in Amazon S3 doesn't encrypt the underlying dataset in Amazon S3.

Athena supports the following S3 encryption options, both for encrypted datasets in Amazon S3 and for encrypted query results:

- Server side encryption with an Amazon S3-managed key (SSE-S3)
- Server-side encryption with a AWS KMS-managed key (SSE-KMS). **Note**
  With SSE-KMS, Athena does not require you to indicate data is encrypted when creating a table.
- Client-side encryption with a AWS KMS-managed key (CSE-KMS)

For more information about AWS KMS encryption with Amazon S3, see What is AWS Key Management Service and How Amazon Simple Storage Service (Amazon S3) Uses AWS KMS in the *AWS Key Management Service Developer Guide*.

Athena does not support SSE with customer-provided keys (SSE-C), nor does it support client-side encryption using a client-side master key. To compare Amazon S3 encryption options, see Protecting Data Using Encryption in the *Amazon Simple Storage Service Developer Guide*.

Athena does not support running queries from one region on encrypted data stored in Amazon S3 in another region.

Permissions for Encrypting and Decrypting Data

If you use SSE-S3 for encryption, Athena users require no additional permissions for encryption and decryption. Having the appropriate Amazon S3 permissions for the appropriate Amazon S3 location (and for Athena actions) is enough. For more information about policies that allow appropriate Athena and Amazon S3 permissions, see IAM Policies for User Access and Amazon S3 Permissions.

For data that is encrypted using AWS KMS, Athena users must be allowed to perform particular AWS KMS actions in addition to Athena and S3 permissions. You allow these actions by editing the key policy for the KMS customer master keys (CMKs) that are used to encrypt data in Amazon S3. The easiest way to do this is to use the IAM console to add key users to the appropriate KMS key policies. For information about how to add a user to a KMS key policy, see How to Modify a Key Policy in the *AWS Key Management Service Developer Guide*.

Note
Advanced key policy administrators may want to fine-tune key policies. `kms:Decrypt` is the minimum allowed action for an Athena user to work with an encrypted dataset. To work with encrypted query results, the minimum allowed actions are `kms:GenerateDataKey` and `kms:Decrypt`.

When using Athena to query datasets in Amazon S3 with a large number of objects that are encrypted with AWS KMS, AWS KMS may throttle query results. This is more likely when there are a large number of small objects. Athena backs off retry requests, but a throttling error might still occur. In this case, visit the AWS Support Center and create a case to increase your limit. For more information about limits and AWS KMS throttling, see Limits in the *AWS Key Management Service Developer Guide*.

Creating Tables Based on Encrypted Datasets in Amazon S3

You indicate to Athena that a dataset is encrypted in Amazon S3 when you create a table (this is not required when using SSE-KMS). For both SSE-S3 and KMS encryption, Athena is able to determine the proper materials to use to decrypt the dataset and create the table, so you don't need to provide key information.

Users that run queries, including the user who creates the table, must have the appropriate permissions as described earlier.

Important
If you use Amazon EMR along with EMRFS to upload encrypted Parquet files, you must disable multipart uploads (set `fs.s3n.multipart.uploads.enabled` to `false`); otherwise, Athena is unable to determine the Parquet file length and a **HIVE_CANNOT_OPEN_SPLIT** error occurs. For more information, see Configure Multipart Upload for Amazon S3 in the *EMR Management Guide*.

Indicate that the dataset is encrypted in Amazon S3 in one of the following ways. This is not required if SSE-KMS is used.

- Use the CREATE TABLE statement with a `TBLPROPERTIES` clause that specifies `'has_encrypted_data'='true'`.

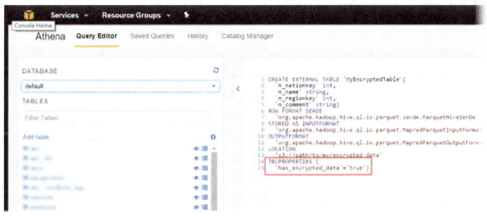

- Use the JDBC driver and set the `TBLPROPERTIES` value as above when you execute CREATE TABLE using `statement.executeQuery()`.
- Use the **Add table** wizard in the Athena console, and then choose **Encrypted data set** when you specify a value for **Location of input data set**.

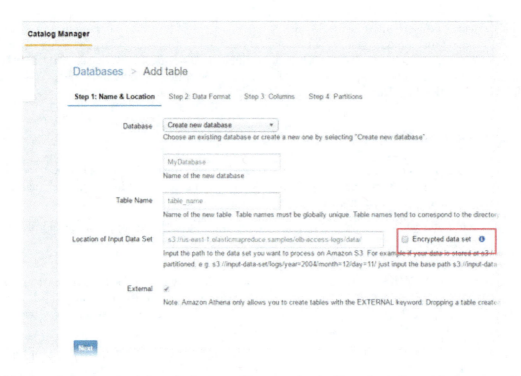

Tables based on encrypted data in Amazon S3 appear in the **Database** list with an encryption icon.

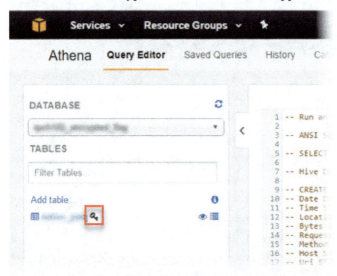

Encrypting Query Results Stored in Amazon S3

You use the Athena console or JDBC driver properties to specify that query results, which Athena stores in the S3 staging directory, are encrypted in Amazon S3. This setting applies to all Athena query results. You can't configure the setting for individual databases, tables, or queries.

To encrypt query results stored in Amazon S3 using the console

1. In the Athena console, choose **Settings**.

2. For **Query result location**, enter a custom value or leave the default. This is the Amazon S3 staging directory where query results are stored.

3. Choose **Encrypt query results**.

4. For **Encryption type**, choose **CSE-KMS**, **SSE-KMS**, or **SSE-S3**.

   If you chose **SSE-KMS** or **CSE-KMS**, for **Encryption key**, specify one of the following:

   - If your account has access to an existing KMS CMK, choose its alias, or
   - Choose **Enter a KMS key ARN** and then enter an ARN.
   - To create a new KMS key, choose **Create KMS key**, use the IAM console to create the key, and then return to specify the key by alias or ARN as described in the previous steps. For more information, see Creating Keys in the *AWS Key Management Service Developer Guide*.

5. Choose **Save**.

Encrypting Query Results stored in Amazon S3 Using the JDBC Driver

You can configure the JDBC Driver to encrypt your query results using any of the encryption protocols that Athena supports. For more information, see the JDBC Driver Installation and Configuration Guide. If you are using the previous version of the driver, see Using Athena with the Previous Version of the JDBC Driver.

Working with Source Data

Amazon Athena supports a subset of data definition language (DDL) statements and ANSI SQL functions and operators to define and query external tables where data resides in Amazon Simple Storage Service.

When you create a database and table in Athena, you describe the schema and the location of the data, making the data in the table ready for read-time querying.

To improve query performance and reduce costs, we recommend that you partition your data and use open source columnar formats for storage in Amazon S3, such as Apache Parquet or ORC.

Topics

- Tables and Databases Creation Process in Athena
- Names for Tables, Databases, and Columns
- Table Location in Amazon S3
- Partitioning Data
- Converting to Columnar Formats

Tables and Databases Creation Process in Athena

You can run DDL statements in the Athena console, using a JDBC or an ODBC driver, or using the Athena **Create Table** wizard.

When you create a new table schema in Athena, Athena stores the schema in a data catalog and uses it when you run queries.

Athena uses an approach known as *schema-on-read*, which means a schema is projected on to your data at the time you execute a query. This eliminates the need for data loading or transformation.

Athena does not modify your data in Amazon S3.

Athena uses Apache Hive to define tables and create databases, which are essentially a logical namespace of tables.

When you create a database and table in Athena, you are simply describing the schema and the location where the table data are located in Amazon S3 for read-time querying. Database and table, therefore, have a slightly different meaning than they do for traditional relational database systems because the data isn't stored along with the schema definition for the database and table.

When you query, you query the table using standard SQL and the data is read at that time. You can find guidance for how to create databases and tables using Apache Hive documentation, but the following provides guidance specifically for Athena.

The maximum query string length is 256 KB.

Hive supports multiple data formats through the use of serializer-deserializer (SerDe) libraries. You can also define complex schemas using regular expressions. For a list of supported SerDe libraries, see Supported Data Formats, SerDes, and Compression Formats.

Requirements for Tables in Athena and Data in Amazon S3

When you create a table, you specify an Amazon S3 bucket location for the underlying data using the `LOCATION` clause. Consider the following:

- You must have the appropriate permissions to work with data in the Amazon S3 location. For more information, see Setting User and Amazon S3 Bucket Permissions.
- If the data is not encrypted in Amazon S3, it can be stored in a different region from the primary region where you run Athena. Standard inter-region data transfer rates for Amazon S3 apply in addition to standard Athena charges.
- If the data is encrypted in Amazon S3, it must be stored in the same region, and the user or principal who creates the table in Athena must have the appropriate permissions to decrypt the data. For more information, see Configuring Encryption Options.
- Athena does not support different storage classes within the bucket specified by the `LOCATION` clause, does not support the `GLACIER` storage class, and does not support Requester Pays buckets. For more information, see Storage Classes, Changing the Storage Class of an Object in Amazon S3, and Requester Pays Buckets in the *Amazon Simple Storage Service Developer Guide*.
- If you issue queries against Amazon S3 buckets with a large number of objects and the data is not partitioned, such queries may affect the Get request rate limits in Amazon S3 and lead to Amazon S3 exceptions. To prevent errors, partition your data. Additionally, consider tuning your Amazon S3 request rates. If your workload in an Amazon S3 bucket routinely exceeds 100 PUT/LIST/DELETE requests per second, or more than 300 GET requests per second, to ensure the best performance and scalability, follow the guidance for tuning performance. For more information, see Request Rate and Performance Considerations.

Functions Supported

The functions supported in Athena queries are those found within Presto. For more information, see Presto 0.172 Functions and Operators in the Presto documentation.

CREATE TABLE AS Type Statements Are Not Supported

Athena does not support CREATE TABLE AS type statements, for example, `CREATE TABLE AS SELECT`, which creates a table from the result of a SELECT query statement.

Transactional Data Transformations Are Not Supported

Athena does not support transaction-based operations (such as the ones found in Hive or Presto) on table data. For a full list of keywords not supported, see Unsupported DDL.

Operations That Change Table States Are ACID

When you create, update, or delete tables, those operations are guaranteed ACID-compliant. For example, if multiple users or clients attempt to create or alter an existing table at the same time, only one will be successful.

All Tables Are EXTERNAL

If you use `CREATE TABLE` without the `EXTERNAL` keyword, Athena issues an error; only tables with the `EXTERNAL` keyword can be created. We recommend that you always use the `EXTERNAL` keyword. When you drop a table in Athena, only the table metadata is removed; the data remains in Amazon S3.

UDF and UDAF Are Not Supported

User-defined functions (UDF or UDAFs) and stored procedures are not supported.

To create a table using the AWS Glue Data Catalog

1. Open the Athena console at https://console.aws.amazon.com/athena/.
2. Choose **AWS Glue Data Catalog**. You can now create a table with the AWS Glue Crawler. For more information, see Using AWS Glue Crawlers.

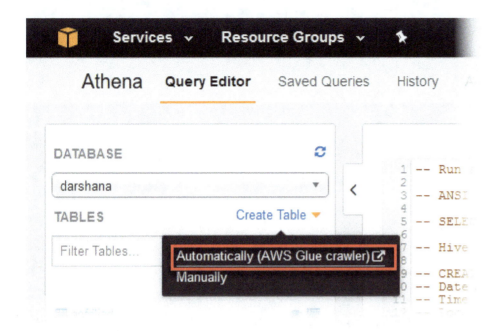

To create a table using the wizard

1. Open the Athena console at https://console.aws.amazon.com/athena/.

2. Under the database display in the Query Editor, choose **Add table**, which displays a wizard.

3. Follow the steps for creating your table.

To create a database using Hive DDL

A database in Athena is a logical grouping for tables you create in it.

1. Open the Athena console at https://console.aws.amazon.com/athena/.

2. Choose **Query Editor**.

3. Enter `CREATE DATABASE myDataBase` and choose **Run Query**.

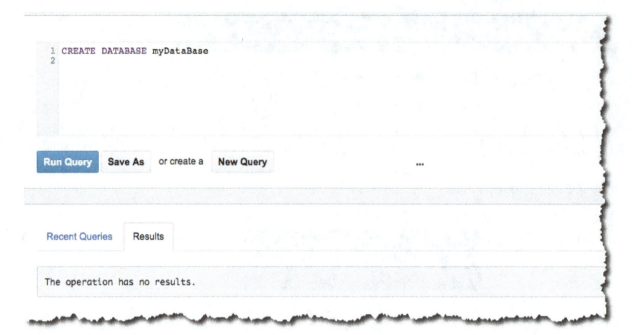

```
1 CREATE DATABASE myDataBase
2
```

Run Query   Save As   or create a   New Query   ...

Recent Queries   Results

The operation has no results.

4. Select your database from the menu. It is likely to be an empty database.

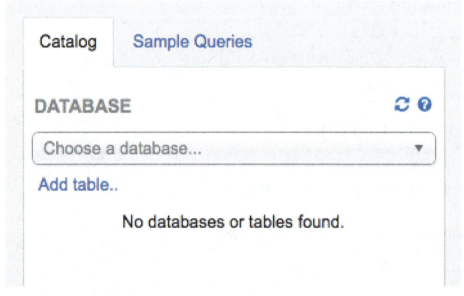

Catalog   Sample Queries

DATABASE

Choose a database...   ▼

Add table..

No databases or tables found.

To create a table using Hive DDL

The Athena Query Editor displays the current database. If you create a table and don't specify a database, the table is created in the database chosen in the **Databases** section on the **Catalog** tab.

1. In the database that you created, create a table by entering the following statement and choosing **Run Query**:

```
1 CREATE EXTERNAL TABLE IF NOT EXISTS cloudfront_logs (
2     `Date` Date,
3     Time STRING,
4     Location STRING,
5     Bytes INT,
6     RequestIP STRING,
```

```
7      Method STRING,
8      Host STRING,
9      Uri STRING,
10     Status INT,
11     Referrer STRING,
12     OS String,
13     Browser String,
14     BrowserVersion String
15  ) ROW FORMAT SERDE 'org.apache.hadoop.hive.serde2.RegexSerDe'
16  WITH SERDEPROPERTIES (
17  "input.regex" = "^(?!#)([^ ]+)\\s+([^ ]+)\\s+([^ ]+)\\s+([^ ]+)\\s+([^ ]+)\\s+([^ ]+)\\s
       +([^ ]+)\\s+([^ ]+)\\s+([^ ]+)\\s+([^ ]+)\\s+[^\(]+[\(]([^\;]+).*\%20([^\/]+)[\/](.*)$"
18  ) LOCATION 's3://athena-examples/cloudfront/plaintext/';
```

2. If the table was successfully created, you can then run queries against your data.

Names for Tables, Databases, and Columns

Use these tips for naming items in Athena.

Table names and table column names in Athena must be lowercase

If you are interacting with Apache Spark, then your table names and table column names must be lowercase. Athena is case-insensitive and turns table names and column names to lower case, but Spark requires lowercase table and column names.

Queries with mixedCase column names, such as `profileURI`, or upper case column names do not work.

Athena table, database, and column names allow only underscore special characters

Athena table, database, and column names cannot contain special characters, other than underscore (_).

Names that begin with an underscore

Use backtics to enclose table or column names that begin with an underscore. For example:

```
1 CREATE TABLE `_myunderscoretable` (
2 `_id` string,
3 `_index`string,
4 ...
```

Table names that include numbers

Enclose table names that include numbers in quotation marks. For example:

```
1 CREATE TABLE "table123"
2 `_id` string,
3 `_index` string,
4 ...
```

Table Location in Amazon S3

When you run a CREATE TABLE AS query in Athena, you register your table with the data catalog that Athena uses. If you migrated to AWS Glue, this is the catalog from AWS Glue. You also specify the location in Amazon S3 for your table in this format: s3://bucketname/keyname.

Use these tips and examples when you specify the location in Amazon S3.

- Athena reads all files in an Amazon S3 location you specify in the CREATE TABLE statement, and cannot ignore any files included in the prefix. When you create tables, include in the Amazon S3 path only the files you want Athena to read. Use AWS Lambda functions to scan files in the source location, remove any empty files, and move unneeded files to another location.
- In the LOCATION clause, use a trailing slash for your folder or bucket.

Use:

```
1 s3://bucketname/prefix/
```

Do not use any of the following items in file locations.

- Do not use filenames, underscores, wildcards, or glob patterns for specifying file locations.
- Do not add the full HTTP notation, such as s3.amazon.com to the Amazon S3 bucket path.

Do not use:

```
1 s3://path_to_bucket
2 s3://path_to_bucket/*
3 s3://path_to_bucket/mySpecialFile.dat
4 s3://bucketname/prefix/filename.csv
5 s3://test-bucket.s3.amazon.com
6 arn:aws:s3:::bucketname/prefix
```

Partitioning Data

By partitioning your data, you can restrict the amount of data scanned by each query, thus improving performance and reducing cost. Athena leverages Hive for partitioning data. You can partition your data by any key. A common practice is to partition the data based on time, often leading to a multi-level partitioning scheme. For example, a customer who has data coming in every hour might decide to partition by year, month, date, and hour. Another customer, who has data coming from many different sources but loaded one time per day, may partition by a data source identifier and date.

If you issue queries against Amazon S3 buckets with a large number of objects and the data is not partitioned, such queries may affect the Get request rate limits in Amazon S3 and lead to Amazon S3 exceptions. To prevent errors, partition your data. Additionally, consider tuning your Amazon S3 request rates. If your workload in an Amazon S3 bucket routinely exceeds 100 PUT/LIST/DELETE requests per second, or more than 300 GET requests per second, to ensure the best performance and scalability, follow the guidance for tuning performance. For more information, see Request Rate and Performance Considerations.

To create a table with partitions, you must define it during the `CREATE TABLE`statement. Use `PARTITIONED BY` to define the keys by which to partition data. There are two scenarios discussed below:

1. Data is already partitioned, stored on Amazon S3, and you need to access the data on Athena.

2. Data is not partitioned.

Scenario 1: Data already partitioned and stored on S3 in hive format

Storing Partitioned Data

Partitions are stored in separate folders in Amazon S3. For example, here is the partial listing for sample ad impressions:

```
1 aws s3 ls s3://elasticmapreduce/samples/hive-ads/tables/impressions/
2
3      PRE dt=2009-04-12-13-00/
4      PRE dt=2009-04-12-13-05/
5      PRE dt=2009-04-12-13-10/
6      PRE dt=2009-04-12-13-15/
7      PRE dt=2009-04-12-13-20/
8      PRE dt=2009-04-12-14-00/
9      PRE dt=2009-04-12-14-05/
10     PRE dt=2009-04-12-14-10/
11     PRE dt=2009-04-12-14-15/
12     PRE dt=2009-04-12-14-20/
13     PRE dt=2009-04-12-15-00/
14     PRE dt=2009-04-12-15-05/
```

Here, logs are stored with the column name (dt) set equal to date, hour, and minute increments. When you give a DDL with the location of the parent folder, the schema, and the name of the partitioned column, Athena can query data in those subfolders.

Creating a Table

To make a table out of this data, create a partition along 'dt' as in the following Athena DDL statement:

```
1 CREATE EXTERNAL TABLE impressions (
2    requestBeginTime string,
```

```
 3      adId string,
 4      impressionId string,
 5      referrer string,
 6      userAgent string,
 7      userCookie string,
 8      ip string,
 9      number string,
10      processId string,
11      browserCookie string,
12      requestEndTime string,
13      timers struct<modelLookup:string, requestTime:string>,
14      threadId string,
15      hostname string,
16      sessionId string)
17 PARTITIONED BY (dt string)
18 ROW FORMAT  serde 'org.apache.hive.hcatalog.data.JsonSerDe'
19     with serdeproperties ( 'paths'='requestBeginTime, adId, impressionId, referrer, userAgent,
            userCookie, ip' )
20 LOCATION 's3://elasticmapreduce/samples/hive-ads/tables/impressions/' ;
```

This table uses Hive's native JSON serializer-deserializer to read JSON data stored in Amazon S3. For more information about the formats supported, see Supported Data Formats, SerDes, and Compression Formats.

After you execute this statement in Athena, choose **New Query** and execute:

```
1 MSCK REPAIR TABLE impressions
```

Athena loads the data in the partitions.

Query the Data

Now, query the data from the impressions table using the partition column. Here's an example:

```
1 SELECT dt,impressionid FROM impressions WHERE dt<'2009-04-12-14-00' and dt>='2009-04-12-13-00'
      ORDER BY dt DESC LIMIT 100
```

This query should show you data similar to the following:

```
 1 2009-04-12-13-20    ap3HcVKAWfXtgIPu6WpuUfAfLODQEc
 2 2009-04-12-13-20    17uchtodoS9kdeQP1x0XThK15IuRsV
 3 2009-04-12-13-20    JOUf1SCtRwviGw8sVcghqE5hOnkgtp
 4 2009-04-12-13-20    NQ2XP0J0dvVbCXJ0pb4XvqJ5A4QxxH
 5 2009-04-12-13-20    fFAItiBMsgqro9kRdIwbeX60SROaxr
 6 2009-04-12-13-20    V4og4R9W6G3QjHHwF7gI1cSqig5D1G
 7 2009-04-12-13-20    hPEPtBwk45msmwWTxPVVo1kVu4v11b
 8 2009-04-12-13-20    vOSkfxegheD90gp31UCr6FplnKpx6i
 9 2009-04-12-13-20    1iD9odVgOIi4QWkwHMcOhmwTkWDKfj
10 2009-04-12-13-20    b31tJiIA25CK8eDHQrHnbcknfSndUk
```

Scenario 2: Data is not partitioned

A layout like the following does not, however, work for automatically adding partition data with MSCK REPAIR TABLE:

```
 1 aws s3 ls s3://athena-examples/elb/plaintext/ --recursive
 2
 3 2016-11-23 17:54:46   11789573 elb/plaintext/2015/01/01/part-r-00000-ce65fca5-d6c6-40e6-b1f9-190
     cc4f93814.txt
 4 2016-11-23 17:54:46    8776899 elb/plaintext/2015/01/01/part-r-00001-ce65fca5-d6c6-40e6-b1f9-190
     cc4f93814.txt
 5 2016-11-23 17:54:46    9309800 elb/plaintext/2015/01/01/part-r-00002-ce65fca5-d6c6-40e6-b1f9-190
     cc4f93814.txt
 6 2016-11-23 17:54:47    9412570 elb/plaintext/2015/01/01/part-r-00003-ce65fca5-d6c6-40e6-b1f9-190
     cc4f93814.txt
 7 2016-11-23 17:54:47   10725938 elb/plaintext/2015/01/01/part-r-00004-ce65fca5-d6c6-40e6-b1f9-190
     cc4f93814.txt
 8 2016-11-23 17:54:46    9439710 elb/plaintext/2015/01/01/part-r-00005-ce65fca5-d6c6-40e6-b1f9-190
     cc4f93814.txt
 9 2016-11-23 17:54:47          0 elb/plaintext/2015/01/01_$folder$
10 2016-11-23 17:54:47    9012723 elb/plaintext/2015/01/02/part-r-00006-ce65fca5-d6c6-40e6-b1f9-190
     cc4f93814.txt
11 2016-11-23 17:54:47    7571816 elb/plaintext/2015/01/02/part-r-00007-ce65fca5-d6c6-40e6-b1f9-190
     cc4f93814.txt
12 2016-11-23 17:54:47    9673393 elb/plaintext/2015/01/02/part-r-00008-ce65fca5-d6c6-40e6-b1f9-190
     cc4f93814.txt
13 2016-11-23 17:54:48   11979218 elb/plaintext/2015/01/02/part-r-00009-ce65fca5-d6c6-40e6-b1f9-190
     cc4f93814.txt
14 2016-11-23 17:54:48    9546833 elb/plaintext/2015/01/02/part-r-00010-ce65fca5-d6c6-40e6-b1f9-190
     cc4f93814.txt
15 2016-11-23 17:54:48   10960865 elb/plaintext/2015/01/02/part-r-00011-ce65fca5-d6c6-40e6-b1f9-190
     cc4f93814.txt
16 2016-11-23 17:54:48          0 elb/plaintext/2015/01/02_$folder$
17 2016-11-23 17:54:48   11360522 elb/plaintext/2015/01/03/part-r-00012-ce65fca5-d6c6-40e6-b1f9-190
     cc4f93814.txt
18 2016-11-23 17:54:48   11211291 elb/plaintext/2015/01/03/part-r-00013-ce65fca5-d6c6-40e6-b1f9-190
     cc4f93814.txt
19 2016-11-23 17:54:48    8633768 elb/plaintext/2015/01/03/part-r-00014-ce65fca5-d6c6-40e6-b1f9-190
     cc4f93814.txt
20 2016-11-23 17:54:49   11891626 elb/plaintext/2015/01/03/part-r-00015-ce65fca5-d6c6-40e6-b1f9-190
     cc4f93814.txt
21 2016-11-23 17:54:49    9173813 elb/plaintext/2015/01/03/part-r-00016-ce65fca5-d6c6-40e6-b1f9-190
     cc4f93814.txt
22 2016-11-23 17:54:49   11899582 elb/plaintext/2015/01/03/part-r-00017-ce65fca5-d6c6-40e6-b1f9-190
     cc4f93814.txt
23 2016-11-23 17:54:49          0 elb/plaintext/2015/01/03_$folder$
24 2016-11-23 17:54:50    8612843 elb/plaintext/2015/01/04/part-r-00018-ce65fca5-d6c6-40e6-b1f9-190
     cc4f93814.txt
25 2016-11-23 17:54:50   10731284 elb/plaintext/2015/01/04/part-r-00019-ce65fca5-d6c6-40e6-b1f9-190
     cc4f93814.txt
26 2016-11-23 17:54:50    9984735 elb/plaintext/2015/01/04/part-r-00020-ce65fca5-d6c6-40e6-b1f9-190
     cc4f93814.txt
27 2016-11-23 17:54:50    9290089 elb/plaintext/2015/01/04/part-r-00021-ce65fca5-d6c6-40e6-b1f9-190
     cc4f93814.txt
28 2016-11-23 17:54:50    7896339 elb/plaintext/2015/01/04/part-r-00022-ce65fca5-d6c6-40e6-b1f9-190
     cc4f93814.txt
29 2016-11-23 17:54:51    8321364 elb/plaintext/2015/01/04/part-r-00023-ce65fca5-d6c6-40e6-b1f9-190
     cc4f93814.txt
30 2016-11-23 17:54:51          0 elb/plaintext/2015/01/04_$folder$
```

31	2016-11-23 17:54:51	7641062	elb/plaintext/2015/01/05/part-r-00024-ce65fca5-d6c6-40e6-b1f9-190
	cc4f93814.txt		
32	2016-11-23 17:54:51	10253377	elb/plaintext/2015/01/05/part-r-00025-ce65fca5-d6c6-40e6-b1f9-190
	cc4f93814.txt		
33	2016-11-23 17:54:51	8502765	elb/plaintext/2015/01/05/part-r-00026-ce65fca5-d6c6-40e6-b1f9-190
	cc4f93814.txt		
34	2016-11-23 17:54:51	11518464	elb/plaintext/2015/01/05/part-r-00027-ce65fca5-d6c6-40e6-b1f9-190
	cc4f93814.txt		
35	2016-11-23 17:54:51	7945189	elb/plaintext/2015/01/05/part-r-00028-ce65fca5-d6c6-40e6-b1f9-190
	cc4f93814.txt		
36	2016-11-23 17:54:51	7864475	elb/plaintext/2015/01/05/part-r-00029-ce65fca5-d6c6-40e6-b1f9-190
	cc4f93814.txt		
37	2016-11-23 17:54:51	0	elb/plaintext/2015/01/05_$folder$
38	2016-11-23 17:54:51	11342140	elb/plaintext/2015/01/06/part-r-00030-ce65fca5-d6c6-40e6-b1f9-190
	cc4f93814.txt		
39	2016-11-23 17:54:51	8063755	elb/plaintext/2015/01/06/part-r-00031-ce65fca5-d6c6-40e6-b1f9-190
	cc4f93814.txt		
40	2016-11-23 17:54:52	9387508	elb/plaintext/2015/01/06/part-r-00032-ce65fca5-d6c6-40e6-b1f9-190
	cc4f93814.txt		
41	2016-11-23 17:54:52	9732343	elb/plaintext/2015/01/06/part-r-00033-ce65fca5-d6c6-40e6-b1f9-190
	cc4f93814.txt		
42	2016-11-23 17:54:52	11510326	elb/plaintext/2015/01/06/part-r-00034-ce65fca5-d6c6-40e6-b1f9-190
	cc4f93814.txt		
43	2016-11-23 17:54:52	9148117	elb/plaintext/2015/01/06/part-r-00035-ce65fca5-d6c6-40e6-b1f9-190
	cc4f93814.txt		
44	2016-11-23 17:54:52	0	elb/plaintext/2015/01/06_$folder$
45	2016-11-23 17:54:52	8402024	elb/plaintext/2015/01/07/part-r-00036-ce65fca5-d6c6-40e6-b1f9-190
	cc4f93814.txt		
46	2016-11-23 17:54:52	8282860	elb/plaintext/2015/01/07/part-r-00037-ce65fca5-d6c6-40e6-b1f9-190
	cc4f93814.txt		
47	2016-11-23 17:54:52	11575283	elb/plaintext/2015/01/07/part-r-00038-ce65fca5-d6c6-40e6-b1f9-190
	cc4f93814.txt		
48	2016-11-23 17:54:53	8149059	elb/plaintext/2015/01/07/part-r-00039-ce65fca5-d6c6-40e6-b1f9-190
	cc4f93814.txt		
49	2016-11-23 17:54:53	10037269	elb/plaintext/2015/01/07/part-r-00040-ce65fca5-d6c6-40e6-b1f9-190
	cc4f93814.txt		
50	2016-11-23 17:54:53	10019678	elb/plaintext/2015/01/07/part-r-00041-ce65fca5-d6c6-40e6-b1f9-190
	cc4f93814.txt		
51	2016-11-23 17:54:53	0	elb/plaintext/2015/01/07_$folder$
52	2016-11-23 17:54:53	0	elb/plaintext/2015/01_$folder$
53	2016-11-23 17:54:53	0	elb/plaintext/2015_$folder$

In this case, you would have to use ALTER TABLE ADD PARTITION to add each partition manually.

For example, to load the data in s3://athena-examples/elb/plaintext/2015/01/01/, you can run the following:

```
1 ALTER TABLE elb_logs_raw_native_part ADD PARTITION (year='2015',month='01',day='01') location '
    s3://athena-examples/elb/plaintext/2015/01/01/'
```

You can also automate adding partitions by using the JDBC driver.

Converting to Columnar Formats

Your Amazon Athena query performance improves if you convert your data into open source columnar formats, such as Apache Parquet or ORC.

You can do this to existing Amazon S3 data sources by creating a cluster in Amazon EMR and converting it using Hive. The following example using the AWS CLI shows you how to do this with a script and data stored in Amazon S3.

Overview

The process for converting to columnar formats using an EMR cluster is as follows:

1. Create an EMR cluster with Hive installed.

2. In the step section of the cluster create statement, specify a script stored in Amazon S3, which points to your input data and creates output data in the columnar format in an Amazon S3 location. In this example, the cluster auto-terminates.

   The full script is located on Amazon S3 at:

```
1 s3://athena-examples/conversion/write-parquet-to-s3.q
```

   Here's an example script beginning with the CREATE TABLE snippet:

```
1  ADD JAR /usr/lib/hive-hcatalog/share/hcatalog/hive-hcatalog-core-1.0.0-amzn-5.jar;
2  CREATE EXTERNAL TABLE impressions (
3    requestBeginTime string,
4    adId string,
5    impressionId string,
6    referrer string,
7    userAgent string,
8    userCookie string,
9    ip string,
10   number string,
11   processId string,
12   browserCookie string,
13   requestEndTime string,
14   timers struct<modelLookup:string, requestTime:string>,
15   threadId string,
16   hostname string,
17   sessionId string)
18 PARTITIONED BY (dt string)
19 ROW FORMAT  serde 'org.apache.hive.hcatalog.data.JsonSerDe'
20 with serdeproperties ( 'paths'='requestBeginTime, adId, impressionId, referrer, userAgent,
       userCookie, ip' )
21 LOCATION 's3://${REGION}.elasticmapreduce/samples/hive-ads/tables/impressions' ;
```

Note
Replace REGION in the LOCATION clause with the region where you are running queries. For example, if your console is in us-east-1, REGION is s3://us-east-1.elasticmapreduce/samples/hive-ads/tables/.

This creates the table in Hive on the cluster which uses samples located in the Amazon EMR samples bucket.

1. On Amazon EMR release 4.7.0, include the ADD JAR line to find the appropriate JsonSerDe. The prettified sample data looks like the following:

```
1 {
2     "number": "977680",
3     "referrer": "fastcompany.com",
4     "processId": "1823",
5     "adId": "TRktxshQXAHWo261jAHubijAoNlAqA",
6     "browserCookie": "mvlrdwrmef",
7     "userCookie": "emFlrLGrm5fA2xLFT5npwbPuG7kf6X",
8     "requestEndTime": "1239714001000",
9     "impressionId": "1I5G2ORmOuG2rt7fFGFgsaWk9Xpkfb",
10    "userAgent": "Mozilla/4.0 (compatible; MSIE 7.0; Windows NT 6.0; SLCC1; .NET CLR
          2.0.50727; Media Center PC 5.0; .NET CLR 3.0.04506; InfoPa",
11    "timers": {
12        "modelLookup": "0.3292",
13        "requestTime": "0.6398"
14    },
15    "threadId": "99",
16    "ip": "67.189.155.225",
17    "modelId": "bxxiuxduad",
18    "hostname": "ec2-0-51-75-39.amazon.com",
19    "sessionId": "J9NOccA3dDMFlixCuSOtl9QBbjs6aS",
20    "requestBeginTime": "1239714000000"
21 }
```

2. In Hive, load the data from the partitions, so the script runs the following:

```
1 MSCK REPAIR TABLE impressions;
```

The script then creates a table that stores your data in a Parquet-formatted file on Amazon S3:

```
1 CREATE EXTERNAL TABLE  parquet_hive (
2     requestBeginTime string,
3     adId string,
4     impressionId string,
5     referrer string,
6     userAgent string,
7     userCookie string,
8     ip string
9 )   STORED AS PARQUET
10 LOCATION 's3://myBucket/myParquet/';
```

The data are inserted from the *impressions* table into *parquet_hive*:

```
1 INSERT OVERWRITE TABLE parquet_hive
2 SELECT
3 requestbegintime,
4 adid,
5 impressionid,
6 referrer,
7 useragent,
8 usercookie,
9 ip FROM impressions WHERE dt='2009-04-14-04-05';
```

The script stores the above *impressions* table columns from the date, 2009-04-14-04-05, into s3://myBucket/myParquet/ in a Parquet-formatted file.

3. After your EMR cluster is terminated, create your table in Athena, which uses the data in the format produced by the cluster.

Before you begin

- You need to create EMR clusters. For more information about Amazon EMR, see the Amazon EMR Management Guide.
- Follow the instructions found in Setting Up.

Example: Converting data to Parquet using an EMR cluster

1. Use the AWS CLI to create a cluster. If you need to install the AWS CLI, see Installing the AWS Command Line Interface in the AWS Command Line Interface User Guide.

2. You need roles to use Amazon EMR, so if you haven't used Amazon EMR before, create the default roles using the following command:

```
1 aws emr create-default-roles
```

3. Create an Amazon EMR cluster using the emr-4.7.0 release to convert the data using the following AWS CLI emr create-cluster command:

```
1  export REGION=us-east-1
2  export SAMPLEURI=s3://${REGION}.elasticmapreduce/samples/hive-ads/tables/impressions/
3  export S3BUCKET=myBucketName
4
5  aws emr create-cluster
6  --applications Name=Hadoop Name=Hive Name=HCatalog \
7  --ec2-attributes KeyName=myKey,InstanceProfile=EMR_EC2_DefaultRole,SubnetId=subnet-
       mySubnetId \
8  --service-role EMR_DefaultRole
9  --release-label emr-4.7.0
10 --instance-type \m4.large
11 --instance-count 1
12 --steps Type=HIVE,Name="Convert to Parquet",\
13 ActionOnFailure=CONTINUE,
14 ActionOnFailure=TERMINATE_CLUSTER,
15 Args=[-f,
16 \s3://athena-examples/conversion/write-parquet-to-s3.q,-hiveconf,
17 INPUT=${SAMPLEURI},-hiveconf,
18 OUTPUT=s3://${S3BUCKET}/myParquet,-hiveconf,
19 REGION=${REGION}
20 ] \
21 --region ${REGION}
22 --auto-terminate
```

For more information, see Create and Use IAM Roles for Amazon EMR in the Amazon EMR Management Guide.

A successful request gives you a cluster ID.

4. Monitor the progress of your cluster using the AWS Management Console, or using the cluster ID with the *list-steps* subcommand in the AWS CLI:

```
1 aws emr list-steps --cluster-id myClusterID
```

Look for the script step status. If it is COMPLETED, then the conversion is done and you are ready to query the data.

1. Create the same table that you created on the EMR cluster.

You can use the same statement as above. Log into Athena and enter the statement in the **Query Editor** window:

```
1 CREATE EXTERNAL TABLE  parquet_hive (
2     requestBeginTime string,
3     adId string,
4     impressionId string,
5     referrer string,
6     userAgent string,
7     userCookie string,
8     ip string
9 )   STORED AS PARQUET
10 LOCATION 's3://myBucket/myParquet/';
```

Choose **Run Query**.

1. Run the following query to show that you can query this data:

```
1 SELECT * FROM parquet_hive LIMIT 10;
```

Alternatively, you can select the view (eye) icon next to the table's name in **Catalog**:

The results should show output similar to this:

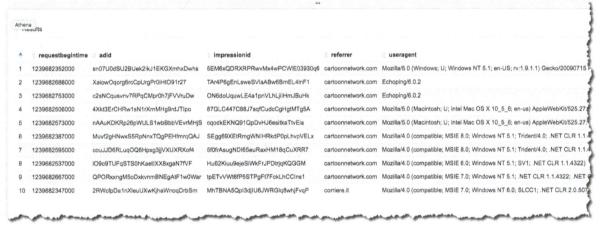

Querying Data in Amazon Athena Tables

Examples of Athena queries in this section show you how to work with arrays, concatenate, filter, flatten, sort, and query data in them. Other examples include queries for data in tables with nested structures and maps, and tables that contain JSON-encoded values.

Topics

- Query Results
- Viewing Query History
- Views
- Querying Arrays
- Querying Arrays with Complex Types and Nested Structures
- Querying Arrays with Maps
- Querying JSON

Query Results

Athena stores query results in Amazon S3.

Each query that you run has:

- A results file stored automatically in a CSV format (*.csv), and
- An Athena metadata file (`*.csv.metadata`).

If necessary, you can access the result files to work with them. Athena stores query results in this Amazon S3 bucket by default: `aws-athena-query-results-<ACCOUNTID>-<REGION>`.

To view or change the default location for saving query results, choose **Settings** in the upper right pane.

Note
You can delete metadata files (`*.csv.metadata`) without causing errors, but important information about the query is lost.

Query results are saved in an Amazon S3 location based on the name of the query and the date the query ran, as follows:

`{QueryLocation}/{QueryName|Unsaved}/{yyyy}/{mm}/{dd}/{QueryID}.csv`

`{QueryLocation}/{QueryName|Unsaved}/{yyyy}/{mm}/{dd}/{QueryID}.csv.metadata`

In this notation:

- `QueryLocation` is the base location for all query results. To view or change this location, choose **Settings**. You can enter a new value for **Query result location** at any time. You can also choose to encrypt query results in Amazon S3. For more information, see Configuring Encryption Options.
- `QueryName` is the name of the query for which the results are saved. If the query wasn't saved, `Unsaved` appears. To see a list of queries and examine their SQL statements, choose **Saved queries**.
- `yyyy/mm/dd/` is the date the query ran.
- `QueryID` is the unique ID of the query.

Saving Query Results

After you run the query, the results appear in the **Results** pane.

To save the results of the most recent query to CSV, choose the file icon.

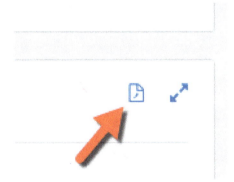

To save the results of a query you ran previously, choose **History**, locate your query, and use **Download Results**.

Viewing Query History

To view your recent query history, use **History**. Athena retains query history for 45 days.

Note
Starting on December 1, 2017, Athena retains query history for 45 days.

To retain query history for a longer period, write a Java program using methods from Athena API and the AWS CLI to periodically retrieve the query history and save it to a data store:

1. Retrieve the query IDs with ListQueryExecutions.

2. Retrieve information about each query based on its ID with GetQueryExecution.

3. Save the obtained information in a data store, such as Amazon S3, using the put-object AWS CLI command from the Amazon S3 API.

Viewing Query History

1. To view a query in your history for up to 45 days after it ran, choose **History** and select a query. You can also see which queries succeeded and failed, download their results, and view query IDs, by clicking the status value.

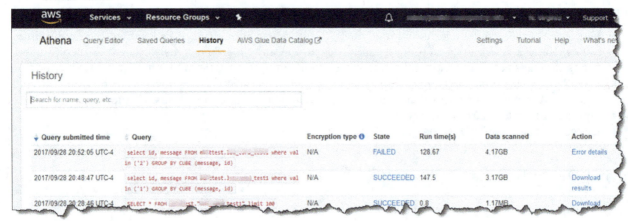

Views

A view in Amazon Athena is a logical, not a physical table. The query that defines a view runs each time the view is referenced in a query.

You can create a view from a `SELECT` query and then reference this view in future queries. For more information, see CREATE VIEW.

Topics

- When to Use Views?
- Supported Actions for Views in Athena
- Working with Views in the Console
- Creating Views
- Examples of Views
- Updating Views
- Deleting Views

When to Use Views?

You may want to create views to:

- *Query a subset of data.* For example, you can create a table with a subset of columns from the original table to simplify querying data.
- *Combine multiple tables in one query.* When you have multiple tables and want to combine them with `UNION ALL`, you can create a view with that expression to simplify queries against the combined tables.
- *Hide the complexity of existing base queries and simplify queries run by users.* Base queries often include joins between tables, expressions in the column list, and other SQL syntax that make it difficult to understand and debug them. You might create a view that hides the complexity and simplifies queries.
- *Experiment with optimization techniques and create optimized queries.* For example, if you find a combination of `WHERE` conditions, `JOIN` order, or other expressions that demonstrate the best performance, you can create a view with these clauses and expressions. Applications can then make relatively simple queries against this view. If you later find a better way to optimize the original query, when you recreate the view, all the applications immediately take advantage of the optimized base query.
- *Hide the underlying table and column names, and minimize maintenance problems* if those names change. In that case, you recreate the view using the new names. All queries that use the view rather than the underlying tables keep running with no changes.

Supported Actions for Views in Athena

Athena supports the following actions for views. You can run these commands in the Query Editor.

Statement	Description
CREATE VIEW	Creates a new view from a specified SELECT query. For more information, see Creating Views. The optional OR REPLACE clause lets you update the existing view by replacing it.
DESCRIBE VIEW	Shows the list of columns for the named view. This allows you to examine the attributes of a complex view.
DROP VIEW	Deletes an existing view. The optional IF EXISTS clause suppresses the error if the view does not exist. For more information, see Deleting Views.
SHOW CREATE VIEW	Shows the SQL statement that creates the specified view.
SHOW VIEWS	Lists the views in the specified database, or in the current database if you omit the database name. Use the optional LIKE clause with a regular expression to restrict the list of view names. You can also see the list of views in the left pane in the console.

Considerations for Views

In Athena, you can preview and work with views created in the Athena Console, in the AWS Glue Data Catalog, if you have migrated to using it, or with Presto running on the Amazon EMR cluster connected to the same catalog. You cannot preview or add to Athena views that were created in other ways.

Athena prevents you from running recursive views and displays an error message in such cases. A recursive view is a view query that references itself.

Athena detects stale views and displays an error message in such cases. A stale view is a view query that references tables or databases that do not exist.

You can create and run nested views as long as the query behind the nested view is valid and the tables and databases exist.

You cannot use views to manage access control on data in Amazon S3. To query a view, you need permissions to access the data stored in Amazon S3. For more information, see Amazon S3 Permissions.

Working with Views in the Console

In the Athena console, you can:

- Locate all views in the left pane, where tables are listed. Athena runs a SHOW VIEWS operation to present this list to you.
- Filter views.
- Preview a view, show its properties, edit it, or delete it.

To list the view actions in the console

A view shows up in the console only if you have already created it.

1. In the Athena console, choose **Views**, choose a view, then expand it.

   The view displays, with the columns it contains, as shown in the following example:

2. In the list of views, choose a view, and open the context (right-click) menu. The actions menu icon () is highlighted for the view that you chose, and the list of actions opens, as shown in the following example:

   http://docs.aws.amazon.com/athena/latest/ug/images/view_options.PNG

3. Choose an option. For example, **Show properties** shows the view name, the name of the database in which the table for the view is created in Athena, and the time stamp when it was created:

   http://docs.aws.amazon.com/athena/latest/ug/images/view_properties.PNG

Creating Views

You can create a view from any **SELECT** query.

To create a view in the console

Before you create a view, choose a database and then choose a table. Run a **SELECT** query on a table and then create a view from it.

1. In the Athena console, choose **Create view**.

   ```
   http://docs.aws.amazon.com/athena/latest/ug/images/create_view.PNG
   ```

   In the Query Editor, a sample view query displays.

2. Edit the sample view query. Specify the table name and add other syntax. For more information, see CREATE VIEW and Examples of Views.

3. Run the view query, debug it if needed, and save it.

Alternatively, create a query in the Query Editor, and then use **Create view from query**.

```
http://docs.aws.amazon.com/athena/latest/ug/images/create_view_from_query.PNG
```

If you run a view that is not valid, Athena displays an error message.

If you delete a table from which the view was created, when you attempt to run the view, Athena displays an error message.

You can create a nested view, which is a view on top of an existing view. Athena prevents you from running a recursive view that references itself.

Examples of Views

To show the syntax of the view query, use SHOW CREATE VIEW.

Example Example 1

Consider the following two tables: a table `employees` with two columns, `id` and `name`, and a table `salaries`, with two columns, `id` and `salary`.

In this example, we create a view named `name_salary` as a SELECT query that obtains a list of IDs mapped to salaries from the tables `employees` and `salaries`:

```
1 CREATE VIEW name_salary AS
2 SELECT
3  employees.name,
4  salaries.salary
5 FROM employees, salaries
6 WHERE employees.id = salaries.id
```

Example Example 2

In the following example, we create a view named `view1` that enables you to hide more complex query syntax. This view runs on top of two tables, `table1` and `table2`, where each table is a different SELECT query. The view selects all columns from `table1` and joins the results with `table2`. The join is based on column `a` that is present in both tables.

```
1  CREATE VIEW view1 AS
2  WITH
3    table1 AS (
4          SELECT a,
5          MAX(b) AS b
6          FROM x
7          GROUP BY a
8          ),
9    table2 AS (
10         SELECT a,
11         AVG(d) AS d
12         FROM y
13         GROUP BY a)
14 SELECT table1.*, table2.*
15 FROM table1
16 JOIN table2
17 ON table1.a = table2.a;
```

Updating Views

After you create a view, it appears in the **Views** list in the left pane.

To edit the view, choose it, choose the context (right-click) menu, and then choose **Show/edit query**. You can also edit the view in the Query Editor. For more information, see CREATE VIEW.

Deleting Views

To delete a view, choose it, choose the context (right-click) menu, and then choose **Delete view**. For more information, see DROP VIEW.

Querying Arrays

Amazon Athena lets you create arrays, concatenate them, convert them to different data types, and then filter, flatten, and sort them.

Topics

- Creating Arrays
- Concatenating Arrays
- Converting Array Data Types
- Finding Lengths
- Accessing Array Elements
- Flattening Nested Arrays
- Creating Arrays from Subqueries
- Filtering Arrays
- Sorting Arrays
- Using Aggregation Functions with Arrays
- Converting Arrays to Strings

Creating Arrays

To build an array literal in Athena, use the **ARRAY** keyword, followed by brackets [ ], and include the array elements separated by commas.

Examples

This query creates one array with four elements.

```
1 SELECT ARRAY [1,2,3,4] AS items
```

It returns:

```
1 +-----------+
2 | items     |
3 +-----------+
4 | [1,2,3,4] |
5 +-----------+
```

This query creates two arrays.

```
1 SELECT ARRAY[ ARRAY[1,2], ARRAY[3,4] ] AS items
```

It returns:

```
1 +-------------------+
2 | items             |
3 +-------------------+
4 | [[1, 2], [3, 4]]  |
5 +-------------------+
```

To create an array from selected columns of compatible types, use a query, as in this example:

```
1 WITH
2 dataset AS (
3   SELECT 1 AS x, 2 AS y, 3 AS z
4 )
5 SELECT ARRAY [x,y,z] AS items FROM dataset
```

This query returns:

```
1 +-----------+
2 | items     |
3 +-----------+
4 | [1,2,3]   |
5 +-----------+
```

In the following example, two arrays are selected and returned as a welcome message.

```
1 WITH
2 dataset AS (
3   SELECT
4     ARRAY ['hello', 'amazon', 'athena'] AS words,
5     ARRAY ['hi', 'alexa'] AS alexa
6 )
7 SELECT ARRAY[words, alexa] AS welcome_msg
8 FROM dataset
```

This query returns:

```
1  +----------------------------------------+
2  | welcome_msg                            |
3  +----------------------------------------+
4  | [[hello, amazon, athena], [hi, alexa]] |
5  +----------------------------------------+
```

To create an array of key-value pairs, use the `MAP` operator that takes an array of keys followed by an array of values, as in this example:

```
1  SELECT ARRAY[
2     MAP(ARRAY['first', 'last', 'age'],ARRAY['Bob', 'Smith', '40']),
3     MAP(ARRAY['first', 'last', 'age'],ARRAY['Jane', 'Doe', '30']),
4     MAP(ARRAY['first', 'last', 'age'],ARRAY['Billy', 'Smith', '8'])
5  ] AS people
```

This query returns:

```
1  +----------------------------------------------------------------------------------------
2  | people

      |
3  +----------------------------------------------------------------------------------------

4  | [{last=Smith, first=Bob, age=40}, {last=Doe, first=Jane, age=30}, {last=Smith, first=Billy,
      age=8}] |
5  +----------------------------------------------------------------------------------------
```

Concatenating Arrays

To concatenate multiple arrays, use the double pipe || operator between them.

```
1 SELECT ARRAY [4,5] || ARRAY[ ARRAY[1,2], ARRAY[3,4] ] AS items
```

This query returns:

```
1 +--------------------------+
2 | items                    |
3 +--------------------------+
4 | [[4, 5], [1, 2], [3, 4]] |
5 +--------------------------+
```

To combine multiple arrays into a single array, use the `concat` function.

```
1 WITH
2 dataset AS (
3   SELECT
4     ARRAY ['hello', 'amazon', 'athena'] AS words,
5     ARRAY ['hi', 'alexa'] AS alexa
6 )
7 SELECT concat(words, alexa) AS welcome_msg
8 FROM dataset
```

This query returns:

```
1 +------------------------------------+
2 | welcome_msg                        |
3 +------------------------------------+
4 | [hello, amazon, athena, hi, alexa] |
5 +------------------------------------+
```

Converting Array Data Types

To convert data in arrays to supported data types, use the `CAST` operator, as `CAST(value AS type)`. Athena supports all of the native Presto data types.

```
1 SELECT
2    ARRAY [CAST(4 AS VARCHAR), CAST(5 AS VARCHAR)]
3 AS items
```

This query returns:

```
1 +-------+
2 | items |
3 +-------+
4 | [4,5] |
5 +-------+
```

Create two arrays with key-value pair elements, convert them to JSON, and concatenate, as in this example:

```
1 SELECT
2    ARRAY[CAST(MAP(ARRAY['a1', 'a2', 'a3'], ARRAY[1, 2, 3]) AS JSON)] ||
3    ARRAY[CAST(MAP(ARRAY['b1', 'b2', 'b3'], ARRAY[4, 5, 6]) AS JSON)]
4 AS items
```

This query returns:

```
1 +---------------------------------------------------+
2 | items                                             |
3 +---------------------------------------------------+
4 | [{"a1":1,"a2":2,"a3":3}, {"b1":4,"b2":5,"b3":6}] |
5 +---------------------------------------------------+
```

Finding Lengths

The `cardinality` function returns the length of an array, as in this example:

```
1  SELECT cardinality(ARRAY[1,2,3,4]) AS item_count
```

This query returns:

```
1  +------------+
2  | item_count |
3  +------------+
4  | 4          |
5  +------------+
```

Accessing Array Elements

To access array elements, use the [] operator, with 1 specifying the first element, 2 specifying the second element, and so on, as in this example:

```
1 WITH dataset AS (
2 SELECT
3   ARRAY[CAST(MAP(ARRAY['a1', 'a2', 'a3'], ARRAY[1, 2, 3]) AS JSON)] ||
4   ARRAY[CAST(MAP(ARRAY['b1', 'b2', 'b3'], ARRAY[4, 5, 6]) AS JSON)]
5 AS items )
6 SELECT items[1] AS item FROM dataset
```

This query returns:

```
1 +-----------------------+
2 | item                  |
3 +-----------------------+
4 | {"a1":1,"a2":2,"a3":3} |
5 +-----------------------+
```

To access the elements of an array at a given position (known as the index position), use the element_at() function and specify the array name and the index position:

- If the index is greater than 0, element_at() returns the element that you specify, counting from the beginning to the end of the array. It behaves as the [] operator.
- If the index is less than 0, element_at() returns the element counting from the end to the beginning of the array.

The following query creates an array words, and selects the first element hello from it as the first_word, the second element amazon (counting from the end of the array) as the middle_word, and the third element athena, as the last_word.

```
1 WITH dataset AS (
2   SELECT ARRAY ['hello', 'amazon', 'athena'] AS words
3 )
4 SELECT
5   element_at(words, 1) AS first_word,
6   element_at(words, -2) AS middle_word,
7   element_at(words, cardinality(words)) AS last_word
8 FROM dataset
```

This query returns:

```
1 +------------------------------------------+
2 | first_word  | middle_word | last_word    |
3 +------------------------------------------+
4 | hello       | amazon      | athena       |
5 +------------------------------------------+
```

Flattening Nested Arrays

When working with nested arrays, you often need to expand nested array elements into a single array, or expand the array into multiple rows.

Examples

To flatten a nested array's elements into a single array of values, use the **flatten** function. This query returns a row for each element in the array.

```
1 SELECT flatten(ARRAY[ ARRAY[1,2], ARRAY[3,4] ]) AS items
```

This query returns:

```
1 +-----------+
2 | items     |
3 +-----------+
4 | [1,2,3,4] |
5 +-----------+
```

To flatten an array into multiple rows, use `CROSS JOIN` in conjunction with the `UNNEST` operator, as in this example:

```
1 WITH dataset AS (
2   SELECT
3     'engineering' as department,
4     ARRAY['Sharon', 'John', 'Bob', 'Sally'] as users
5 )
6 SELECT department, names FROM dataset
7 CROSS JOIN UNNEST(users) as t(names)
```

This query returns:

```
1  +----------------------+
2  | department | names   |
3  +----------------------+
4  | engineering | Sharon |
5  +----------------------|
6  | engineering | John   |
7  +----------------------|
8  | engineering | Bob    |
9  +----------------------|
10 | engineering | Sally  |
11 +----------------------+
```

To flatten an array of key-value pairs, transpose selected keys into columns, as in this example:

```
1 WITH
2 dataset AS (
3   SELECT
4     'engineering' as department,
5     ARRAY[
6       MAP(ARRAY['first', 'last', 'age'],ARRAY['Bob', 'Smith', '40']),
7       MAP(ARRAY['first', 'last', 'age'],ARRAY['Jane', 'Doe', '30']),
8       MAP(ARRAY['first', 'last', 'age'],ARRAY['Billy', 'Smith', '8'])
9     ] AS people
```

```
10  )
11 SELECT names['first'] AS
12  first_name,
13  names['last'] AS last_name,
14  department FROM dataset
15 CROSS JOIN UNNEST(people) AS t(names)
```

This query returns:

```
1 +------------------------------------+
2 | first_name | last_name | department  |
3 +------------------------------------+
4 | Bob        | Smith     | engineering |
5 | Jane       | Doe       | engineering |
6 | Billy      | Smith     | engineering |
7 +------------------------------------+
```

From a list of employees, select the employee with the highest combined scores. UNNEST can be used in the FROM clause without a preceding CROSS JOIN as it is the default join operator and therefore implied.

```
1 WITH
2 dataset AS (
3   SELECT ARRAY[
4     CAST(ROW('Sally', 'engineering', ARRAY[1,2,3,4]) AS ROW(name VARCHAR, department VARCHAR,
          scores ARRAY(INTEGER))),
5     CAST(ROW('John', 'finance', ARRAY[7,8,9]) AS ROW(name VARCHAR, department VARCHAR, scores
          ARRAY(INTEGER))),
6     CAST(ROW('Amy', 'devops', ARRAY[12,13,14,15]) AS ROW(name VARCHAR, department VARCHAR,
          scores ARRAY(INTEGER)))
7   ] AS users
8 ),
9 users AS (
10  SELECT person, score
11  FROM
12    dataset,
13    UNNEST(dataset.users) AS t(person),
14    UNNEST(person.scores) AS t(score)
15 )
16 SELECT person.name, person.department, SUM(score) AS total_score FROM users
17 GROUP BY (person.name, person.department)
18 ORDER BY (total_score) DESC
19 LIMIT 1
```

This query returns:

```
1 +----------------------------------+
2 | name | department | total_score |
3 +----------------------------------+
4 | Amy  | devops     | 54          |
5 +----------------------------------+
```

From a list of employees, select the employee with the highest individual score.

```
1 WITH
2 dataset AS (
3   SELECT ARRAY[
```

```
4      CAST(ROW('Sally', 'engineering', ARRAY[1,2,3,4]) AS ROW(name VARCHAR, department VARCHAR,
          scores ARRAY(INTEGER))),
5      CAST(ROW('John', 'finance', ARRAY[7,8,9]) AS ROW(name VARCHAR, department VARCHAR, scores
          ARRAY(INTEGER))),
6      CAST(ROW('Amy', 'devops', ARRAY[12,13,14,15]) AS ROW(name VARCHAR, department VARCHAR, scores
          ARRAY(INTEGER)))
7    ] AS users
8  ),
9  users AS (
10   SELECT person, score
11   FROM
12     dataset,
13     UNNEST(dataset.users) AS t(person),
14     UNNEST(person.scores) AS t(score)
15 )
16 SELECT person.name, score FROM users
17 ORDER BY (score) DESC
18 LIMIT 1
```

This query returns:

```
1  +---------------+
2  | name | score |
3  +---------------+
4  | Amy  | 15    |
5  +---------------+
```

Creating Arrays from Subqueries

Create an array from a collection of rows.

```
1 WITH
2 dataset AS (
3   SELECT ARRAY[1,2,3,4,5] AS items
4 )
5 SELECT array_agg(i) AS array_items
6 FROM dataset
7 CROSS JOIN UNNEST(items) AS t(i)
```

This query returns:

```
1 +-----------------+
2 | array_items     |
3 +-----------------+
4 | [1, 2, 3, 4, 5] |
5 +-----------------+
```

To create an array of unique values from a set of rows, use the **distinct** keyword.

```
1 WITH
2 dataset AS (
3   SELECT ARRAY [1,2,2,3,3,4,5] AS items
4 )
5 SELECT array_agg(distinct i) AS array_items
6 FROM dataset
7 CROSS JOIN UNNEST(items) AS t(i)
```

This query returns the following result. Note that ordering is not guaranteed.

```
1 +-----------------+
2 | array_items     |
3 +-----------------+
4 | [1, 2, 3, 4, 5] |
5 +-----------------+
```

Filtering Arrays

Create an array from a collection of rows if they match the filter criteria.

```
1 WITH
2 dataset AS (
3   SELECT ARRAY[1,2,3,4,5] AS items
4 )
5 SELECT array_agg(i) AS array_items
6 FROM dataset
7 CROSS JOIN UNNEST(items) AS t(i)
8 WHERE i > 3
```

This query returns:

```
1 +--------------+
2 | array_items |
3 +--------------+
4 | [4, 5]      |
5 +--------------+
```

Filter an array based on whether one of its elements contain a specific value, such as 2, as in this example:

```
1  WITH
2  dataset AS (
3    SELECT ARRAY
4    [
5      ARRAY[1,2,3,4],
6      ARRAY[5,6,7,8],
7      ARRAY[9,0]
8    ] AS items
9  )
10 SELECT i AS array_items FROM dataset
11 CROSS JOIN UNNEST(items) AS t(i)
12 WHERE contains(i, 2)
```

This query returns:

```
1 +---------------+
2 | array_items   |
3 +---------------+
4 | [1, 2, 3, 4] |
5 +---------------+
```

Sorting Arrays

Create a sorted array of unique values from a set of rows.

```
1 WITH
2 dataset AS (
3   SELECT ARRAY[3,1,2,5,2,3,6,3,4,5] AS items
4 )
5 SELECT array_sort(array_agg(distinct i)) AS array_items
6 FROM dataset
7 CROSS JOIN UNNEST(items) AS t(i)
```

This query returns:

```
1 +--------------------+
2 | array_items        |
3 +--------------------+
4 | [1, 2, 3, 4, 5, 6] |
5 +--------------------+
```

Using Aggregation Functions with Arrays

- To add values within an array, use SUM, as in the following example.
- To aggregate multiple rows within an array, use `array_agg`. For information, see Creating Arrays from Subqueries.

```
1  WITH
2  dataset AS (
3    SELECT ARRAY
4    [
5      ARRAY[1,2,3,4],
6      ARRAY[5,6,7,8],
7      ARRAY[9,0]
8    ] AS items
9  ),
10 item AS (
11   SELECT i AS array_items
12   FROM dataset, UNNEST(items) AS t(i)
13 )
14 SELECT array_items, sum(val) AS total
15 FROM item, UNNEST(array_items) AS t(val)
16 GROUP BY array_items
```

This query returns the following results. The order of returned results is not guaranteed.

```
1  +----------------------+
2  | array_items | total |
3  +----------------------+
4  | [1, 2, 3, 4] | 10    |
5  | [5, 6, 7, 8] | 26    |
6  | [9, 0]       | 9     |
7  +----------------------+
```

Converting Arrays to Strings

To convert an array into a single string, use the `array_join` function.

```
1 WITH
2 dataset AS (
3   SELECT ARRAY ['hello', 'amazon', 'athena'] AS words
4 )
5 SELECT array_join(words, ' ') AS welcome_msg
6 FROM dataset
```

This query returns:

```
1 +---------------------+
2 | welcome_msg         |
3 +---------------------+
4 | hello amazon athena |
5 +---------------------+
```

Querying Arrays with Complex Types and Nested Structures

Your source data often contains arrays with complex data types and nested structures. Examples in this section show how to change element's data type, locate elements within arrays, order values, and find keywords using Athena queries.

- Creating a ROW
- Changing Field Names in Arrays Using CAST
- Filtering Arrays Using the . Notation
- Filtering Arrays with Nested Values
- Filtering Arrays Using UNNEST
- Finding Keywords in Arrays
- Ordering Values in Arrays

Creating a ROW

Note

The examples in this section use ROW as a means to create sample data to work with. When you query tables within Athena, you do not need to create ROW data types, as they are already created from your data source by Presto. When you use CREATE_TABLE, Athena defines a STRUCT in it, and relies on Presto for populating it with data. In turn, Presto creates the ROW data type for you, for each row in the dataset. The underlying ROW data type consists of named fields of any SQL data types supported in Presto.

```
1 WITH dataset AS (
2   SELECT
3     ROW('Bob', 38) AS users
4   )
5 SELECT * FROM dataset
```

This query returns:

```
1 +--------------------------+
2 | users                    |
3 +--------------------------+
4 | {field0=Bob, field1=38}  |
5 +--------------------------+
```

Changing Field Names in Arrays Using CAST

To change the field name in an array that contains ROW values, you can CAST the ROW declaration:

```
1 WITH dataset AS (
2   SELECT
3     CAST(
4       ROW('Bob', 38) AS ROW(name VARCHAR, age INTEGER)
5     ) AS users
6 )
7 SELECT * FROM dataset
```

This query returns:

```
1 +--------------------+
2 | users              |
3 +--------------------+
```

116

```
4 | {NAME=Bob, AGE=38} |
5 +--------------------+
```

Note

In the example above, you declare `name` as a `VARCHAR` because this is its type in Presto. If you declare this `STRUCT` inside a `CREATE TABLE` statement, use `String` type because Hive defines this data type as `String`.

Filtering Arrays Using the . Notation

In the following example, select the `accountId` field from the `userIdentity` column of a AWS CloudTrail logs table by using the dot . notation. For more information, see Querying AWS CloudTrail Logs.

```
1 SELECT
2   CAST(useridentity.accountid AS bigint) as newid
3 FROM cloudtrail_logs
4 LIMIT 2;
```

This query returns:

```
1 +---------------+
2 | newid         |
3 +---------------+
4 | 112233445566  |
5 +---------------+
6 | 998877665544  |
7 +---------------+
```

To query an array of values, issue this query:

```
1 WITH dataset AS (
2   SELECT ARRAY[
3     CAST(ROW('Bob', 38) AS ROW(name VARCHAR, age INTEGER)),
4     CAST(ROW('Alice', 35) AS ROW(name VARCHAR, age INTEGER)),
5     CAST(ROW('Jane', 27) AS ROW(name VARCHAR, age INTEGER))
6   ] AS users
7 )
8 SELECT * FROM dataset
```

It returns this result:

```
1 +-------------------------------------------------------------------+
2 | users                                                             |
3 +-------------------------------------------------------------------+
4 | [{NAME=Bob, AGE=38}, {NAME=Alice, AGE=35}, {NAME=Jane, AGE=27}]   |
5 +-------------------------------------------------------------------+
```

Filtering Arrays with Nested Values

Large arrays often contain nested structures, and you need to be able to filter, or search, for values within them.

To define a dataset for an array of values that includes a nested `BOOLEAN` value, issue this query:

```
1 WITH dataset AS (
2   SELECT
3     CAST(
```

```
4      ROW('aws.amazon.com', ROW(true)) AS ROW(hostname VARCHAR, flaggedActivity ROW(isNew
            BOOLEAN))
5    ) AS sites
6 )
7 SELECT * FROM dataset
```

It returns this result:

```
1 +-------------------------------------------------------------+
2 | sites                                                       |
3 +-------------------------------------------------------------+
4 | {HOSTNAME=aws.amazon.com, FLAGGEDACTIVITY={ISNEW=true}}     |
5 +-------------------------------------------------------------+
```

Next, to filter and access the BOOLEAN value of that element, continue to use the dot . notation.

```
1 WITH dataset AS (
2   SELECT
3     CAST(
4       ROW('aws.amazon.com', ROW(true)) AS ROW(hostname VARCHAR, flaggedActivity ROW(isNew
            BOOLEAN))
5     ) AS sites
6 )
7 SELECT sites.hostname, sites.flaggedactivity.isnew
8 FROM dataset
```

This query selects the nested fields and returns this result:

```
1 +------------------------+
2 | hostname      | isnew |
3 +------------------------+
4 | aws.amazon.com | true |
5 +------------------------+
```

Filtering Arrays Using UNNEST

To filter an array that includes a nested structure by one of its child elements, issue a query with an UNNEST operator. For more information about UNNEST, see Flattening Nested Arrays.

For example, this query finds hostnames of sites in the dataset.

```
1 WITH dataset AS (
2   SELECT ARRAY[
3     CAST(
4       ROW('aws.amazon.com', ROW(true)) AS ROW(hostname VARCHAR, flaggedActivity ROW(isNew
            BOOLEAN))
5     ),
6     CAST(
7       ROW('news.cnn.com', ROW(false)) AS ROW(hostname VARCHAR, flaggedActivity ROW(isNew BOOLEAN
            ))
8     ),
9     CAST(
10      ROW('netflix.com', ROW(false)) AS ROW(hostname VARCHAR, flaggedActivity ROW(isNew BOOLEAN)
            )
11    )
12  ] as items
```

```
13 )
14 SELECT sites.hostname, sites.flaggedActivity.isNew
15 FROM dataset, UNNEST(items) t(sites)
16 WHERE sites.flaggedActivity.isNew = true
```

It returns:

```
1 +------------------------+
2 | hostname       | isnew |
3 +------------------------+
4 | aws.amazon.com | true  |
5 +------------------------+
```

Finding Keywords in Arrays

To search a dataset for a keyword within an element inside an array, use the `regexp_like` function.

Consider an array of sites containing their hostname, and a `flaggedActivity` element. This element includes an `ARRAY`, containing several `MAP` elements, each listing different popular keywords and their popularity count. Assume you want to find a particular keyword inside a `MAP` in this array.

To search this dataset for sites with a specific keyword, use the `regexp_like` function.

Note

Instead of using the SQL LIKE operator, this query uses the `regexp_like` function. This function takes as an input a regular expression pattern to evaluate, or a list of terms separated by |, known as an `OR` operator. Additionally, searching for a large number of keywords is more efficient with the `regexp_like` function, because its performance exceeds that of the SQL LIKE operator.

```
1  WITH dataset AS (
2    SELECT ARRAY[
3      CAST(
4        ROW('aws.amazon.com', ROW(ARRAY[
5            MAP(ARRAY['term', 'count'], ARRAY['bigdata', '10']),
6            MAP(ARRAY['term', 'count'], ARRAY['serverless', '50']),
7            MAP(ARRAY['term', 'count'], ARRAY['analytics', '82']),
8            MAP(ARRAY['term', 'count'], ARRAY['iot', '74'])
9        ])
10       ) AS ROW(hostname VARCHAR, flaggedActivity ROW(flags ARRAY(MAP(VARCHAR, VARCHAR)) ))
11     ),
12     CAST(
13       ROW('news.cnn.com', ROW(ARRAY[
14         MAP(ARRAY['term', 'count'], ARRAY['politics', '241']),
15         MAP(ARRAY['term', 'count'], ARRAY['technology', '211']),
16         MAP(ARRAY['term', 'count'], ARRAY['serverless', '25']),
17         MAP(ARRAY['term', 'count'], ARRAY['iot', '170'])
18       ])
19       ) AS ROW(hostname VARCHAR, flaggedActivity ROW(flags ARRAY(MAP(VARCHAR, VARCHAR)) ))
20     ),
21     CAST(
22       ROW('netflix.com', ROW(ARRAY[
23         MAP(ARRAY['term', 'count'], ARRAY['cartoons', '1020']),
24         MAP(ARRAY['term', 'count'], ARRAY['house of cards', '112042']),
25         MAP(ARRAY['term', 'count'], ARRAY['orange is the new black', '342']),
26         MAP(ARRAY['term', 'count'], ARRAY['iot', '4'])
27       ])
```

```
28        ) AS ROW(hostname VARCHAR, flaggedActivity ROW(flags ARRAY(MAP(VARCHAR, VARCHAR)) ))
29    )
30  ] AS items
31 ),
32 sites AS (
33   SELECT sites.hostname, sites.flaggedactivity
34   FROM dataset, UNNEST(items) t(sites)
35 )
36 SELECT hostname
37 FROM sites, UNNEST(sites.flaggedActivity.flags) t(flags)
38 WHERE regexp_like(flags['term'], 'politics|bigdata')
39 GROUP BY (hostname)
```

This query returns two sites:

```
1 +----------------+
2 | hostname       |
3 +----------------+
4 | aws.amazon.com |
5 +----------------+
6 | news.cnn.com   |
7 +----------------+
```

Ordering Values in Arrays

To order values in an array, use ORDER BY. The query in the following example adds up the total popularity scores for the sites matching your search terms with the regexp_like function, and then orders them from highest to lowest.

```
1  WITH dataset AS (
2    SELECT ARRAY[
3      CAST(
4        ROW('aws.amazon.com', ROW(ARRAY[
5            MAP(ARRAY['term', 'count'], ARRAY['bigdata', '10']),
6            MAP(ARRAY['term', 'count'], ARRAY['serverless', '50']),
7            MAP(ARRAY['term', 'count'], ARRAY['analytics', '82']),
8            MAP(ARRAY['term', 'count'], ARRAY['iot', '74'])
9        ])
10       ) AS ROW(hostname VARCHAR, flaggedActivity ROW(flags ARRAY(MAP(VARCHAR, VARCHAR)) ))
11   ),
12     CAST(
13       ROW('news.cnn.com', ROW(ARRAY[
14         MAP(ARRAY['term', 'count'], ARRAY['politics', '241']),
15         MAP(ARRAY['term', 'count'], ARRAY['technology', '211']),
16         MAP(ARRAY['term', 'count'], ARRAY['serverless', '25']),
17         MAP(ARRAY['term', 'count'], ARRAY['iot', '170'])
18       ])
19       ) AS ROW(hostname VARCHAR, flaggedActivity ROW(flags ARRAY(MAP(VARCHAR, VARCHAR)) ))
20   ),
21     CAST(
22       ROW('netflix.com', ROW(ARRAY[
23         MAP(ARRAY['term', 'count'], ARRAY['cartoons', '1020']),
24         MAP(ARRAY['term', 'count'], ARRAY['house of cards', '112042']),
25         MAP(ARRAY['term', 'count'], ARRAY['orange is the new black', '342']),
```

```
26        MAP(ARRAY['term', 'count'], ARRAY['iot', '4'])
27      ])
28      ) AS ROW(hostname VARCHAR, flaggedActivity ROW(flags ARRAY(MAP(VARCHAR, VARCHAR)) ))
29    )
30  ] AS items
31 ),
32 sites AS (
33   SELECT sites.hostname, sites.flaggedactivity
34   FROM dataset, UNNEST(items) t(sites)
35 )
36 SELECT hostname, array_agg(flags['term']) AS terms, SUM(CAST(flags['count'] AS INTEGER)) AS
      total
37 FROM sites, UNNEST(sites.flaggedActivity.flags) t(flags)
38 WHERE regexp_like(flags['term'], 'politics|bigdata')
39 GROUP BY (hostname)
40 ORDER BY total DESC
```

This query returns this result:

```
1 +-------------------------------------------------+
2 | hostname       | terms               | total |
3 +-------------------------------------------------+
4 | news.cnn.com   | [politics,serverless] | 241   |
5 +-------------------------------------------------+
6 | aws.amazon.com | [serverless]        | 10    |
7 +-------------------------------------------------+
```

Querying Arrays with Maps

Maps are key-value pairs that consist of data types available in Athena.

To create maps, use the MAP operator and pass it two arrays: the first is the column (key) names, and the second is values. All values in the arrays must be of the same type. If any of the map value array elements need to be of different types, you can convert them later.

Examples

This example selects a user from a dataset. It uses the MAP operator and passes it two arrays. The first array includes values for column names, such as "first", "last", and "age". The second array consists of values for each of these columns, such as "Bob", "Smith", "35".

```
1 WITH dataset AS (
2   SELECT MAP(
3     ARRAY['first', 'last', 'age'],
4     ARRAY['Bob', 'Smith', '35']
5   ) AS user
6 )
7 SELECT user FROM dataset
```

This query returns:

```
1 +----------------------------------+
2 | user                             |
3 +----------------------------------+
4 | {last=Smith, first=Bob, age=35}  |
5 +----------------------------------+
```

You can retrieve Map values by selecting the field name followed by [key_name], as in this example:

```
1 WITH dataset AS (
2   SELECT MAP(
3     ARRAY['first', 'last', 'age'],
4     ARRAY['Bob', 'Smith', '35']
5   ) AS user
6 )
7 SELECT user['first'] AS first_name FROM dataset
```

This query returns:

```
1 +------------+
2 | first_name |
3 +------------+
4 | Bob        |
5 +------------+
```

Querying JSON

Amazon Athena lets you parse JSON-encoded values, extract data from JSON, search for values, and find length and size of JSON arrays.

Topics

- Best Practices for Reading JSON Data
- Extracting Data from JSON
- Searching for Values
- Obtaining Length and Size of JSON Arrays

Best Practices for Reading JSON Data

JavaScript Object Notation (JSON) is a common method for encoding data structures as text. Many applications and tools output data that is JSON-encoded.

In Amazon Athena, you can create tables from external data and include the JSON-encoded data in them. For such types of source data, use Athena together with JSON SerDe Libraries.

Use the following tips to read JSON-encoded data:

- Choose the right SerDe, a native JSON SerDe, `org.apache.hive.hcatalog.data.JsonSerDe`, or an OpenX SerDe, `org.openx.data.jsonserde.JsonSerDe`. For more information, see JSON SerDe Libraries.

- Make sure that each JSON-encoded record is represented on a separate line.

- Generate your JSON-encoded data in case-insensitive columns.

- Provide an option to ignore malformed records, as in this example.

```
1  CREATE EXTERNAL TABLE json_table (
2    column_a string
3    column_b int
4  )
5  ROW FORMAT SERDE 'org.openx.data.jsonserde.JsonSerDe'
6  WITH SERDEPROPERTIES ('ignore.malformed.json' = 'true')
7  LOCATION 's3://bucket/path/';
```

- Convert fields in source data that have an undetermined schema to JSON-encoded strings in Athena.

When Athena creates tables backed by JSON data, it parses the data based on the existing and predefined schema. However, not all of your data may have a predefined schema. To simplify schema management in such cases, it is often useful to convert fields in source data that have an undetermined schema to JSON strings in Athena, and then use JSON SerDe Libraries.

For example, consider an IoT application that publishes events with common fields from different sensors. One of those fields must store a custom payload that is unique to the sensor sending the event. In this case, since you don't know the schema, we recommend that you store the information as a JSON-encoded string. To do this, convert data in your Athena table to JSON, as in the following example. You can also convert JSON-encoded data to Athena data types.

- Converting Athena Data Types to JSON
- Converting JSON to Athena Data Types

Converting Athena Data Types to JSON

To convert Athena data types to JSON, use `CAST`.

```
1  WITH dataset AS (
2    SELECT
3      CAST('HELLO ATHENA' AS JSON) AS hello_msg,
4      CAST(12345 AS JSON) AS some_int,
5      CAST(MAP(ARRAY['a', 'b'], ARRAY[1,2]) AS JSON) AS some_map
6  )
7  SELECT * FROM dataset
```

This query returns:

```
1  +-----------------------------------------------+
2  | hello_msg      | some_int | some_map          |
```

```
3 +----------------------------------------------+
4 | "HELLO ATHENA" | 12345     | {"a":1,"b":2} |
5 +----------------------------------------------+
```

Converting JSON to Athena Data Types

To convert JSON data to Athena data types, use `CAST`.

Note
In this example, to denote strings as JSON-encoded, start with the `JSON` keyword and use single quotes, such as
`JSON '12345'`

```
1 WITH dataset AS (
2   SELECT
3     CAST(JSON '"HELLO ATHENA"' AS VARCHAR) AS hello_msg,
4     CAST(JSON '12345' AS INTEGER) AS some_int,
5     CAST(JSON '{"a":1,"b":2}' AS MAP(VARCHAR, INTEGER)) AS some_map
6 )
7 SELECT * FROM dataset
```

This query returns:

```
1 +----------------------------------------+
2 | hello_msg     | some_int | some_map   |
3 +----------------------------------------+
4 | HELLO ATHENA | 12345     | {a:1,b:2} |
5 +----------------------------------------+
```

Extracting Data from JSON

You may have source data with containing JSON-encoded strings that you do not necessarily want to deserialize into a table in Athena. In this case, you can still run SQL operations on this data, using the JSON functions available in Presto.

Consider this JSON string as an example dataset.

```
1 {"name": "Susan Smith",
2 "org": "engineering",
3 "projects":
4     [
5      {"name":"project1", "completed":false},
6      {"name":"project2", "completed":true}
7     ]
8 }
```

Examples: extracting properties

To extract the `name` and `projects` properties from the JSON string, use the `json_extract` function as in the following example. The `json_extract` function takes the column containing the JSON string, and searches it using a `JSONPath`-like expression with the dot . notation.

Note
`JSONPath` performs a simple tree traversal. It uses the `$` sign to denote the root of the JSON document, followed by a period and an element nested directly under the root, such as `$.name`.

```
1  WITH dataset AS (
2    SELECT '{"name": "Susan Smith",
3           "org": "engineering",
4           "projects": [{"name":"project1", "completed":false},
5           {"name":"project2", "completed":true}]}'
6      AS blob
7  )
8  SELECT
9    json_extract(blob, '$.name') AS name,
10   json_extract(blob, '$.projects') AS projects
11 FROM dataset
```

The returned value is a JSON-encoded string, and not a native Athena data type.

```
1 +---------------------------------------------------------------------------------------+
2 | name           | projects
    |
3 +---------------------------------------------------------------------------------------+
4 | "Susan Smith"  | [{"name":"project1","completed":false},{"name":"project2","completed":true}]
    |
5 +---------------------------------------------------------------------------------------+
```

To extract the scalar value from the JSON string, use the `json_extract_scalar` function. It is similar to `json_extract`, but returns only scalar values (Boolean, number, or string).

Note

Do not use the `json_extract_scalar` function on arrays, maps, or structs.

```
1 WITH dataset AS (
2   SELECT '{"name": "Susan Smith",
3           "org": "engineering",
4           "projects": [{"name":"project1", "completed":false},{"name":"project2", "completed":
            true}]}'
5     AS blob
6 )
7 SELECT
8   json_extract_scalar(blob, '$.name') AS name,
9   json_extract_scalar(blob, '$.projects') AS projects
10 FROM dataset
```

This query returns:

```
1 +---------------------------+
2 | name          | projects |
3 +---------------------------+
4 | Susan Smith   |          |
5 +---------------------------+
```

To obtain the first element of the `projects` property in the example array, use the `json_array_get` function and specify the index position.

```
1 WITH dataset AS (
2   SELECT '{"name": "Bob Smith",
3           "org": "engineering",
4           "projects": [{"name":"project1", "completed":false},{"name":"project2", "completed":
            true}]}'
5     AS blob
6 )
7 SELECT json_array_get(json_extract(blob, '$.projects'), 0) AS item
8 FROM dataset
```

It returns the value at the specified index position in the JSON-encoded array.

```
1 +---------------------------------------+
2 | item                                  |
3 +---------------------------------------+
4 | {"name":"project1","completed":false} |
5 +---------------------------------------+
```

To return an Athena string type, use the `[]` operator inside a `JSONPath` expression, then Use the `json_extract_scalar` function. For more information about `[]`, see Accessing Array Elements.

```
1 WITH dataset AS (
2   SELECT '{"name": "Bob Smith",
3           "org": "engineering",
4           "projects": [{"name":"project1", "completed":false},{"name":"project2", "completed
            ":true}]}'
5     AS blob
6 )
7 SELECT json_extract_scalar(blob, '$.projects[0].name') AS project_name
8 FROM dataset
```

It returns this result:

```
1  +--------------+
2  | project_name |
3  +--------------+
4  | project1     |
5  +--------------+
```

Searching for Values

To determine if a specific value exists inside a JSON-encoded array, use the `json_array_contains` function.

The following query lists the names of the users who are participating in "project2".

```
1 WITH dataset AS (
2   SELECT * FROM (VALUES
3     (JSON '{"name": "Bob Smith", "org": "legal", "projects": ["project1"]}'),
4     (JSON '{"name": "Susan Smith", "org": "engineering", "projects": ["project1", "project2", "
        project3"]}'),
5     (JSON '{"name": "Jane Smith", "org": "finance", "projects": ["project1", "project2"]}')
6   ) AS t (users)
7 )
8 SELECT json_extract_scalar(users, '$.name') AS user
9 FROM dataset
10 WHERE json_array_contains(json_extract(users, '$.projects'), 'project2')
```

This query returns a list of users.

```
1 +-------------+
2 | user        |
3 +-------------+
4 | Susan Smith |
5 +-------------+
6 | Jane Smith  |
7 +-------------+
```

The following query example lists the names of users who have completed projects along with the total number of completed projects. It performs these actions:

- Uses nested `SELECT` statements for clarity.
- Extracts the array of projects.
- Converts the array to a native array of key-value pairs using `CAST`.
- Extracts each individual array element using the `UNNEST` operator.
- Filters obtained values by completed projects and counts them.

Note

When using `CAST` to `MAP` you can specify the key element as `VARCHAR` (native String in Presto), but leave the value as JSON, because the values in the `MAP` are of different types: String for the first key-value pair, and Boolean for the second.

```
1 WITH dataset AS (
2   SELECT * FROM (VALUES
3     (JSON '{"name": "Bob Smith",
4              "org": "legal",
5              "projects": [{"name":"project1", "completed":false}]}'),
6     (JSON '{"name": "Susan Smith",
7              "org": "engineering",
8              "projects": [{"name":"project2", "completed":true},
9                          {"name":"project3", "completed":true}]}'),
10    (JSON '{"name": "Jane Smith",
11            "org": "finance",
12            "projects": [{"name":"project2", "completed":true}]}')
13  ) AS t (users)
14 ),
15 employees AS (
```

```
16    SELECT users, CAST(json_extract(users, '$.projects') AS
17      ARRAY(MAP(VARCHAR, JSON))) AS projects_array
18    FROM dataset
19  ),
20  names AS (
21    SELECT json_extract_scalar(users, '$.name') AS name, projects
22    FROM employees, UNNEST (projects_array) AS t(projects)
23  )
24  SELECT name, count(projects) AS completed_projects FROM names
25  WHERE cast(element_at(projects, 'completed') AS BOOLEAN) = true
26  GROUP BY name
```

This query returns the following result:

```
1 +----------------------------------+
2 | name          | completed_projects |
3 +----------------------------------+
4 | Susan Smith | 2                |
5 +----------------------------------+
6 | Jane Smith  | 1                |
7 +----------------------------------+
```

Obtaining Length and Size of JSON Arrays

Example: `json_array_length`

To obtain the length of a JSON-encoded array, use the `json_array_length` function.

```
1  WITH dataset AS (
2    SELECT * FROM (VALUES
3      (JSON '{"name":
4              "Bob Smith",
5              "org":
6              "legal",
7              "projects": [{"name":"project1", "completed":false}]}'),
8      (JSON '{"name": "Susan Smith",
9              "org": "engineering",
10             "projects": [{"name":"project2", "completed":true},
11                          {"name":"project3", "completed":true}]}'),
12     (JSON '{"name": "Jane Smith",
13             "org": "finance",
14             "projects": [{"name":"project2", "completed":true}]}')
15   ) AS t (users)
16 )
17 SELECT
18   json_extract_scalar(users, '$.name') as name,
19   json_array_length(json_extract(users, '$.projects')) as count
20 FROM dataset
21 ORDER BY count DESC
```

This query returns this result:

```
1  +--------------------+
2  | name         | count |
3  +--------------------+
4  | Susan Smith | 2     |
5  +--------------------+
6  | Bob Smith   | 1     |
7  +--------------------+
8  | Jane Smith  | 1     |
9  +--------------------+
```

Example: `json_size`

To obtain the size of a JSON-encoded array or object, use the `json_size` function, and specify the column containing the JSON string and the `JSONPath` expression to the array or object.

```
1  WITH dataset AS (
2    SELECT * FROM (VALUES
3      (JSON '{"name": "Bob Smith", "org": "legal", "projects": [{"name":"project1", "completed":
           false}]}'),
4      (JSON '{"name": "Susan Smith", "org": "engineering", "projects": [{"name":"project2", "
           completed":true},{"name":"project3", "completed":true}]}'),
5      (JSON '{"name": "Jane Smith", "org": "finance", "projects": [{"name":"project2", "completed
           ":true}]}')
6    ) AS t (users)
```

```
 7 )
 8 SELECT
 9   json_extract_scalar(users, '$.name') as name,
10   json_size(users, '$.projects') as count
11 FROM dataset
12 ORDER BY count DESC
```

This query returns this result:

```
1 +--------------------+
2 | name         | count |
3 +--------------------+
4 | Susan Smith | 2     |
5 +--------------------+
6 | Bob Smith   | 1     |
7 +--------------------+
8 | Jane Smith  | 1     |
9 +--------------------+
```

Querying Geospatial Data

Geospatial data contains identifiers that specify a geographic position for an object. Examples of this type of data include weather reports, map directions, tweets with geographic positions, store locations, and airline routes. Geospatial data plays an important role in business analytics, reporting, and forecasting.

Geospatial identifiers, such as latitude and longitude, allow you to convert any mailing address into a set of geographic coordinates.

Topics

- What is a Geospatial Query?
- Input Data Formats and Geometry Data Types
- List of Supported Geospatial Functions
- Examples: Geospatial Queries

What is a Geospatial Query?

Geospatial queries are specialized types of SQL queries supported in Athena. They differ from non-spatial SQL queries in the following ways:

- Using the following specialized geometry data types: `point`, `line`, `multiline`, `polygon`, and `multipolygon`.
- Expressing relationships between geometry data types, such as `distance`, `equals`, `crosses`, `touches`, `overlaps`, `disjoint`, and others.

Using geospatial queries in Athena, you can run these and other similar operations:

- Find the distance between two points.
- Check whether one area (polygon) contains another.
- Check whether one line crosses or touches another line or polygon.

For example, to obtain a point type from a pair of `double` values for the geographic coordinates of Mount Rainier in Athena, use the `ST_POINT (double, double)((longitude, latitude)pair)` geospatial function, specifying the latitude and longitude:

```
1 ST_POINT(46.8527,-121.7602) ((longitude, latitude) pair)
```

Input Data Formats and Geometry Data Types

To use geospatial functions in Athena, input your data in the WKT or WKB formats, or use the Hive JSON SerDe. You can also use the geometry data types supported in Athena.

Input Data Formats

To handle geospatial queries, Athena supports input data in these data formats:

- **WKT (Well-known Text)**. In Athena, WKT is represented as a `varchar` data type.
- **WKB (Well-known binary)**. In Athena, WKB is represented as a `varbinary` data type with a spatial reference ID (WKID) 4326. For information about both of these types, see the Wikipedia topic on Well-known text.
- **JSON-encoded geospatial data**. To parse JSON files with geospatial data and create tables for them, Athena uses the Hive JSON SerDe. For more information about using this SerDe in Athena, see JSON SerDe Libraries.

Geometry Data Types

To handle geospatial queries, Athena supports these specialized geometry data types:

- `point`
- `line`
- `polygon`
- `multiline`
- `multipolygon`

List of Supported Geospatial Functions

Geospatial functions in Athena have these characteristics:

- The functions follow the general principles of Spatial Query.
- The functions are implemented as a Presto plugin that uses the ESRI Java Geometry Library. This library has an Apache 2 license.
- The functions rely on the ESRI Geometry API.
- Not all of the ESRI-supported functions are available in Athena. This topic lists only the ESRI geospatial functions that are supported in Athena.

Athena supports four types of geospatial functions:

- Constructor Functions
- Geospatial Relationship Functions
- Operation Functions
- Accessor Functions

Before You Begin

Create two tables, `earthquakes` and `counties`, as follows:

```
1 CREATE external TABLE earthquakes
2 (
3  earthquake_date STRING,
4  latitude DOUBLE,
5  longitude DOUBLE,
6  depth DOUBLE,
7  magnitude DOUBLE,
8  magtype string,
9  mbstations string,
10  gap string,
11  distance string,
12  rms string,
13  source string,
14  eventid string
15 )
16 ROW FORMAT DELIMITED FIELDS TERMINATED BY ','
17 STORED AS TEXTFILE LOCATION 's3://my-query-log/csv'
```

```
1 CREATE external TABLE IF NOT EXISTS counties
2  (
3  Name string,
4  BoundaryShape binary
5  )
6 ROW FORMAT SERDE 'com.esri.hadoop.hive.serde.JsonSerde'
7 STORED AS INPUTFORMAT 'com.esri.json.hadoop.EnclosedJsonInputFormat'
8 OUTPUTFORMAT 'org.apache.hadoop.hive.ql.io.HiveIgnoreKeyTextOutputFormat'
9 LOCATION 's3://my-query-log/json'
```

Some of the subsequent examples are based on these tables and rely on two sample files stored in the Amazon S3 location. These files are not inlcuded with Athena and are used for illustration purposes only:

- An `earthquakes.csv` file, which lists earthquakes that occurred in California. This file has fields that correspond to the fields in the table `earthquakes`.

- A `california-counties.json` file, which lists JSON-encoded county data in the ESRI-compliant format, and includes many fields, such as AREA, PERIMETER, STATE, COUNTY, and NAME. The `counties` table is based on this file and has two fields only: `Name` (string), and `BoundaryShape` (binary).

Constructor Functions

Use constructor geospatial functions to obtain binary representations of a `point`, "line, orpolygon". You can also convert a particular geometry data type to text, and obtain a binary representation of a geometry data type from text (WKT).

ST_POINT(double, double)

Returns a value in the `point` data type, which is a binary representation of the geometry data type `point`.

Syntax:

```
1 SELECT ST_POINT(longitude, latitude)
2 FROM earthquakes
3 LIMIT 1;
```

In the alternative syntax, you can also specify the coordinates as a `point` data type with two values:

```
1 SELECT ST_POINT('point (0 0)')
2 FROM earthquakes
3 LIMIT 1;
```

Example. This example uses specific longitude and latitude coordinates from `earthquakes.csv`:

```
1 SELECT ST_POINT(61.56, -158.54)
2 FROM earthquakes
3 LIMIT 1;
```

It returns this binary representation of a geometry data type `point`:

```
1 00 00 00 00 01 01 00 00 00 48 e1 7a 14 ae c7 4e 40 e1 7a 14 ae 47 d1 63 c0
```

ST_LINE(varchar)

Returns a value in the `line` data type, which is a binary representation of the geometry data type `line`. Example:

```
1 SELECT ST_Line('linestring(1 1, 2 2, 3 3)')
```

ST_POLYGON(varchar)

Returns a value in the `polygon` data type, which is a binary representation of the geometry data type `polygon`. Example:

```
1 SELECT ST_Polygon('polygon ((1 1, 4 1, 1 4))')
```

ST_GEOMETRY_TO_TEXT (varbinary)

Converts each of the specified geometry data types to text. Returns a value in a geometry data type, which is a WKT representation of the geometry data type. Example:

```
1 SELECT ST_GEOMETRY_TO_TEXT(ST_POINT(61.56, -158.54))
```

`ST_GEOMETRY_FROM_TEXT (varchar)`

Converts text into a geometry data type. Returns a value in a geometry data type, which is a binary representation of the geometry data type. Example:

```
1 SELECT ST_GEOMETRY_FROM_TEXT(ST_GEOMETRY_TO_TEXT(ST_Point(1, 2)))
```

Geospatial Relationship Functions

The following functions express relationships between two different geometries that you specify as input. They return results of type `boolean`. The order in which you specify the pair of geometries matters: the first geometry value is called the left geometry, the second geometry value is called the right geometry.

These functions return:

- `TRUE` if and only if the relationship described by the function is satisfied.
- `FALSE` if and only if the relationship described by the function is not satisfied.

`ST_CONTAINS (geometry, geometry)`

Returns `TRUE` if and only if the left geometry contains the right geometry. Examples:

```
1 SELECT ST_CONTAINS('POLYGON((0 2,1 1,0 -1,0 2))', 'POLYGON((-1 3,2 1,0 -3,-1 3))')
```

```
1 SELECT ST_CONTAINS('POLYGON((0 2,1 1,0 -1,0 2))', ST_Point(0, 0));
```

```
1 SELECT ST_CONTAINS(ST_GEOMETRY_FROM_TEXT('POLYGON((0 2,1 1,0 -1,0 2))'), ST_GEOMETRY_FROM_TEXT('
    POLYGON((-1 3,2 1,0 -3,-1 3))'))
```

`ST_CROSSES (geometry, geometry)`

Returns `TRUE` if and only if the left geometry crosses the right geometry. Example:

```
1 SELECT ST_CROSSES(ST_LINE('linestring(1 1, 2 2 )'), ST_LINE('linestring(0 1, 2 2)'))
```

`ST_DISJOINT (geometry, geometry)`

Returns `TRUE` if and only if the intersection of the left geometry and the right geometry is empty. Example:

```
1 SELECT ST_DISJOINT(ST_LINE('linestring(0 0, 0 1)'), ST_LINE('linestring(1 1, 1 0)'))
```

`ST_EQUALS (geometry, geometry)`

Returns `TRUE` if and only if the left geometry equals the right geometry. Example:

```
1 SELECT ST_EQUALS(ST_LINE('linestring( 0 0, 1 1)'), ST_LINE('linestring(1 3, 2 2)'))
```

`ST_INTERSECTS (geometry, geometry)`

Returns `TRUE` if and only if the left geometry intersects the right geometry. Example:

```
1 SELECT ST_INTERSECTS(ST_LINE('linestring(8 7, 7 8)'), ST_POLYGON('polygon((1 1, 4 1, 4 4, 1 4))
    '))
```

ST_OVERLAPS (geometry, geometry)

Returns TRUE if and only if the left geometry overlaps the right geometry. Example:

```
1 SELECT ST_OVERLAPS(ST_POLYGON('polygon((2 0, 2 1, 3 1))'), ST_POLYGON('polygon((1 1, 1 4, 4 4, 4
      1))'))
```

ST_RELATE (geometry, geometry)

Returns TRUE if and only if the left geometry has the specified Dimensionally Extended nine-Intersection Model (DE-9IM) relationship with the right geometry. For more information, see the Wikipedia topic DE-9IM. Example:

```
1 SELECT ST_RELATE(ST_LINE('linestring(0 0, 3 3)'), ST_LINE('linestring(1 1, 4 4)'), 'T********')
```

ST_TOUCHES (geometry, geometry)

Returns TRUE if and only if the left geometry touches the right geometry.

Example:

```
1 SELECT ST_TOUCHES(ST_POINT(8, 8), ST_POLYGON('polygon((1  1, 1  4, 4  4, 4 1))'))
```

ST_WITHIN (geometry, geometry)

Returns TRUE if and only if the left geometry is within the right geometry.

Example:

```
1 SELECT ST_WITHIN(ST_POINT(8, 8), ST_POLYGON('polygon((1  1, 1  4, 4  4, 4 1))'))
```

Operation Functions

Use operation functions to perform operations on geometry data type values. For example, you can obtain the boundaries of a single geometry data type; intersections between two geometry data types; difference between left and right geometries, where each is of the same geometry data type; or an exterior buffer or ring around a particular geometry data type.

All operation functions take as an input one of the geometry data types and return their binary representations.

ST_BOUNDARY (geometry)

Takes as an input one of the geometry data types, and returns a binary representation of the **boundary** geometry data type.

Examples:

```
1 SELECT ST_BOUNDARY(ST_LINE('linestring(0 1, 1 0)')))
```

```
1 SELECT ST_BOUNDARY(ST_POLYGON('polygon((1  1, 1  4, 4  4, 4 1))'))
```

ST_BUFFER (geometry, double)

Takes as an input a geometry data type and a distance (as type `double`). Returns a binary representation of the geometry data type buffered by the specified distance.

Example:

```
1 SELECT ST_BUFFER(ST_Point(1, 2), 2.0)
```

ST_DIFFERENCE (geometry, geometry)

Returns a binary representation of a difference between the left geometry and right geometry. Example:

```
1 SELECT ST_GEOMETRY_TO_TEXT(ST_DIFFERENCE(ST_POLYGON('polygon((0 0, 0 10, 10 10, 10 0))'),
    ST_POLYGON('polygon((0 0, 0 5, 5 5, 5 0))')))
```

ST_ENVELOPE (geometry)

Takes as an input one of the geometry data types and returns a binary representation of an envelope, where an envelope is a rectangle around the specified geometry data type. Examples:

```
1 SELECT ST_ENVELOPE(ST_LINE('linestring(0 1, 1 0)'))
```

```
1 SELECT ST_ENVELOPE(ST_POLYGON('polygon((1 1, 1 4, 4 4, 4 1))'))
```

ST_EXTERIOR_RING (geometry)

Returns a binary representation of the exterior ring of the input type `polygon`. Examples:

```
1 SELECT ST_EXTERIOR_RING(ST_POLYGON(1,1, 1,4, 4,1))
```

```
1 SELECT ST_EXTERIOR_RING(ST_POLYGON('polygon ((0 0, 8 0, 0 8, 0 0), (1 1, 1 5, 5 1, 1 1))'))
```

ST_INTERSECTION (geometry, geometry)

Returns a binary representation of the intersection of the left geometry and right geometry. Examples:

```
1 SELECT ST_INTERSECTION(ST_POINT(1,1), ST_POINT(1,1))
```

```
1 SELECT ST_INTERSECTION(ST_LINE('linestring(0 1, 1 0)'), ST_POLYGON('polygon((1 1, 1 4, 4 4, 4
    1))'))
```

```
1 SELECT ST_GEOMETRY_TO_TEXT(ST_INTERSECTION(ST_POLYGON('polygon((2 0, 2 3, 3 0))'), ST_POLYGON('
    polygon((1 1, 4 1, 4 4, 1 4))')))
```

ST_SYMMETRIC_DIFFERENCE (geometry, geometry)

Returns a binary representation of the geometrically symmetric difference between left geometry and right geometry. Example:

```
1 SELECT ST_GEOMETRY_TO_TEXT(ST_SYMMETRIC_DIFFERENCE(ST_LINE('linestring(0 2, 2 2)'), ST_LINE('
    linestring(1 2, 3 2)')))
```

Accessor Functions

Accessor functions are useful to obtain values in types `varchar`, `bigint`, or `double` from different `geometry` data types, where `geometry` is any of the geometry data types supported in Athena: `point`, `line`, `polygon`, `multiline`, and `multipolygon`. For example, you can obtain an area of a `polygon` geometry data type, maximum and minimum X and Y values for a specified geometry data type, obtain the length of a `line`, or receive the number of points in a specified geometry data type.

ST_AREA (geometry)

Takes as an input a geometry data type `polygon` and returns an area in type `double`. Example:

```
1 SELECT ST_AREA(ST_POLYGON('polygon((1 1, 4 1, 4 4, 1 4))'))
```

ST_CENTROID (geometry)

Takes as an input a geometry data type `polygon`, and returns a `point` that is the center of the polygon's envelope in type `varchar`. Example:

```
1 SELECT ST_CENTROID(ST_GEOMETRY_FROM_TEXT('polygon ((0 0, 3 6, 6 0, 0 0))'))
```

ST_COORDINATE_DIMENSION (geometry)

Takes as input one of the supported geometry types, and returns the count of coordinate components in type `bigint`. Example:

```
1 SELECT ST_COORDINATE_DIMENSION(ST_POINT(1.5,2.5))
```

ST_DIMENSION (geometry)

Takes as an input one of the supported geometry types, and returns the spatial dimension of a geometry in type `bigint`. Example:

```
1 SELECT ST_DIMENSION(ST_POLYGON('polygon((1 1, 4 1, 4 4, 1 4))'))
```

ST_DISTANCE (geometry, geometry)

Returns the distance in type `double` between the left geometry and the right geometry. Example:

```
1 SELECT ST_DISTANCE(ST_POINT(0.0,0.0), ST_POINT(3.0,4.0))
```

ST_IS_CLOSED (geometry)

Returns TRUE (type `boolean`) if and only if the line is closed. Example:

```
1 SELECT ST_IS_CLOSED(ST_LINE('linestring(0 2, 2 2)'))
```

ST_IS_EMPTY (geometry)

Returns TRUE (type boolean) if and only if the specified geometry is empty. Example:

```
1 SELECT ST_IS_EMPTY(ST_POINT(1.5, 2.5))
```

ST_IS_RING (geometry)

Returns TRUE (type boolean) if and only if the line type is closed and simple. Example:

```
1 SELECT ST_IS_RING(ST_LINE('linestring(0 2, 2 2)'))
```

ST_LENGTH (geometry)

Returns the length of line in type double. Example:

```
1 SELECT ST_LENGTH(ST_LINE('linestring(0 2, 2 2)'))
```

ST_MAX_X (geometry)

Returns the maximum X coordinate of a geometry in type double. Example:

```
1 SELECT ST_MAX_X(ST_LINE('linestring(0 2, 2 2)'))
```

ST_MAX_Y (geometry)

Returns the maximum Y coordinate of a geometry in type double. Example:

```
1 SELECT ST_MAX_Y(ST_LINE('linestring(0 2, 2 2)'))
```

ST_MIN_X (geometry)

Returns the minimum X coordinate of a geometry in type double. Example:

```
1 SELECT ST_MIN_X(ST_LINE('linestring(0 2, 2 2)'))
```

ST_MIN_Y (geometry)

Returns the minimum Y coordinate of a geometry in type double. Example:

```
1 SELECT ST_MAX_Y(ST_LINE('linestring(0 2, 2 2)'))
```

ST_START_POINT (geometry)

Returns the first point of a line geometry data type in type point. Example:

```
1 SELECT ST_START_POINT(ST_LINE('linestring(0 2, 2 2)'))
```

ST_END_POINT (geometry)

Returns the last point of a `line` geometry data type in type `point`. Example:

```
1 SELECT ST_END_POINT(ST_LINE('linestring(0 2, 2 2)'))
```

ST_X (point)

Returns the X coordinate of a point in type `double`. Example:

```
1 SELECT ST_X(ST_POINT(1.5, 2.5))
```

ST_Y (point)

Returns the Y coordinate of a point in type `double`. Example:

```
1 SELECT ST_Y(ST_POINT(1.5, 2.5))
```

ST_POINT_NUMBER (geometry)

Returns the number of points in the geometry in type `bigint`. Example:

```
1 SELECT ST_POINT_NUMBER(ST_POINT(1.5, 2.5))
```

ST_INTERIOR_RING_NUMBER (geometry)

Returns the number of interior rings in the `polygon` geometry in type `bigint`. Example:

```
1 SELECT ST_INTERIOR_RING_NUMBER(ST_POLYGON('polygon ((0 0, 8 0, 0 8, 0 0), (1 1, 1 5, 5 1, 1 1))
    '))
```

Examples: Geospatial Queries

The following examples create two tables and issue a query against them.

These examples rely on two files stored in an Amazon S3 location:

- An `earthquakes.csv` sample file, which lists earthquakes that occurred in California. This file has fields that correspond to the fields in the table `earthquakes` in the following example.
- A `california-counties.json` file, which lists JSON-encoded county data in the ESRI-compliant format, and includes many fields, such as AREA, PERIMETER, STATE, COUNTY, and NAME. The following example shows the `counties` table from this file with two fields only: `Name` (string), and `BoundaryShape` (binary).

Note

These files contain sample data and are not guaranteed to be accurate. They are used in the documentation for illustration purposes only and are not included with the product.

The following code example creates a table called `earthquakes`:

```
1  CREATE external TABLE earthquakes
2  (
3   earthquake_date STRING,
4   latitude DOUBLE,
5   longitude DOUBLE,
6   depth DOUBLE,
7   magnitude DOUBLE,
8   magtype string,
9   mbstations string,
10  gap string,
11  distance string,
12  rms string,
13  source string,
14  eventid string
15 )
16 ROW FORMAT DELIMITED FIELDS TERMINATED BY ','
17 STORED AS TEXTFILE LOCATION 's3://my-query-log/csv'
```

The following code example creates a table called `counties`:

```
1  CREATE external TABLE IF NOT EXISTS counties
2   (
3   Name string,
4   BoundaryShape binary
5   )
6  ROW FORMAT SERDE 'com.esri.hadoop.hive.serde.JsonSerde'
7  STORED AS INPUTFORMAT 'com.esri.json.hadoop.EnclosedJsonInputFormat'
8  OUTPUTFORMAT 'org.apache.hadoop.hive.ql.io.HiveIgnoreKeyTextOutputFormat'
9  LOCATION 's3://my-query-log/json'
```

The following code example uses the `CROSS JOIN` function for the two tables created earlier. Additionally, for both tables, it uses `ST_CONTAINS` and asks for counties whose boundaries include a geographical location of the earthquakes, specified with `ST_POINT`. It then groups such counties by name, orders them by count, and returns them.

```
1  SELECT counties.name,
2        COUNT(*) cnt
3  FROM counties
4  CROSS JOIN earthquakes
```

```
5 WHERE ST_CONTAINS (counties.boundaryshape, ST_POINT(earthquakes.longitude, earthquakes.latitude)
       )
6 GROUP BY  counties.name
7 ORDER BY  cnt DESC
```

This query returns:

```
1  +------------------------+
2  | name            | cnt |
3  +------------------------+
4  | Kern            | 36  |
5  +------------------------+
6  | San Bernardino  | 35  |
7  +------------------------+
8  | Imperial        | 28  |
9  +------------------------+
10 | Inyo            | 20  |
11 +------------------------+
12 | Los Angeles     | 18  |
13 +------------------------+
14 | Riverside       | 14  |
15 +------------------------+
16 | Monterey        | 14  |
17 +------------------------+
18 | Santa Clara     | 12  |
19 +------------------------+
20 | San Benito      | 11  |
21 +------------------------+
22 | Fresno          | 11  |
23 +------------------------+
24 | San Diego       | 7   |
25 +------------------------+
26 | Santa Cruz      | 5   |
27 +------------------------+
28 | Ventura         | 3   |
29 +------------------------+
30 | San Luis Obispo | 3   |
31 +------------------------+
32 | Orange          | 2   |
33 +------------------------+
34 | San Mateo       | 1   |
35 +------------------------+
```

Querying AWS Service Logs

This section includes several procedures for using Amazon Athena to query popular datasets, such as AWS CloudTrail logs, Amazon CloudFront logs, Classic Load Balancer logs, Application Load Balancer logs, and Amazon VPC flow logs.

The tasks in this section use the Athena console, but you can also use other tools that connect via JDBC. For more information, see Accessing Amazon Athena with JDBC, the AWS CLI, or the Amazon Athena API Reference.

The topics in this section assume that you have set up both an IAM user with appropriate permissions to access Athena and the Amazon S3 bucket where the data to query should reside. For more information, see Setting Up and Getting Started.

Topics

- Querying AWS CloudTrail Logs
- Querying Amazon CloudFront Logs
- Querying Classic Load Balancer Logs
- Querying Application Load Balancer Logs
- Querying Amazon VPC Flow Logs

Querying AWS CloudTrail Logs

AWS CloudTrail is a service that records AWS API calls and events for AWS accounts.

CloudTrail logs include details about any API calls made to your AWS services, including the console. CloudTrail generates encrypted log files and stores them in Amazon S3. For more information, see the AWS CloudTrail User Guide.

Using Athena with CloudTrail logs is a powerful way to enhance your analysis of AWS service activity. For example, you can use queries to identify trends and further isolate activity by attributes, such as source IP address or user.

A common application is to use CloudTrail logs to analyze operational activity for security and compliance. For information about a detailed example, see the AWS Big Data Blog post, Analyze Security, Compliance, and Operational Activity Using AWS CloudTrail and Amazon Athena.

You can use Athena to query these log files directly from Amazon S3, specifying the `LOCATION` of log files. You can do this one of two ways:

- By creating tables for CloudTrail log files directly from the CloudTrail console.
- By manually creating tables for CloudTrail log files in the Athena console.

Topics

- Understanding CloudTrail Logs and Athena Tables
- Creating a Table for CloudTrail Logs in the CloudTrail Console
- Manually Creating the Table for CloudTrail Logs in Athena
- Tips for Querying CloudTrail Logs

Understanding CloudTrail Logs and Athena Tables

Before you begin creating tables, you should understand a little more about CloudTrail and how it stores data. This can help you create the tables that you need, whether you create them from the CloudTrail console or from Athena.

CloudTrail saves logs as JSON text files`in compressed gzip format (*.json.gzip). The location of the log files depends on how you set up trails, the AWS Region or Regions in which you are logging, and other factors.

For more information about where logs are stored, the JSON structure, and the record file contents, see the following topics in the AWS CloudTrail User Guide:

- Finding Your CloudTrail Log Files
- CloudTrail Log File Examples
- CloudTrail Record Contents
- CloudTrail Event Reference

To collect logs and save them to Amazon S3, enable CloudTrail for the console. For more information, see Creating a Trail in the *AWS CloudTrail User Guide.*

Note the destination Amazon S3 bucket where you save the logs. Replace the `LOCATION` clause with the path to the CloudTrail log location and the set of objects with which to work. The example uses a `LOCATION` value of logs for a particular account, but you can use the degree of specificity that suits your application.

For example:

- To analyze data from multiple accounts, you can roll back the `LOCATION` specifier to indicate all `AWSLogs` by using `LOCATION 's3://MyLogFiles/AWSLogs/`.
- To analyze data from a specific date, account, and Region, use `LOCATION` s3://MyLogFiles/123456789012/CloudTrail/us-east-1/2016/03/14/'.'

Using the highest level in the object hierarchy gives you the greatest flexibility when you query using Athena.

Creating a Table for CloudTrail Logs in the CloudTrail Console

You can automatically create tables for querying CloudTrail logs directly from the CloudTrail console. This is a fairly straightforward method of creating tables, but you can only create tables this way if the Amazon S3 bucket that contains the log files for the trail is in a Region supported by Amazon Athena, and you are logged in with an IAM user or role that has sufficient permissions to create tables in Athena. For more information, see Setting Up.

To create a table for a CloudTrail trail in the CloudTrail console

1. Open the CloudTrail console at https://console.aws.amazon.com/cloudtrail/.

2. In the navigation pane, choose **Event history**.

3. In **Event history**, choose **Run advanced queries in Amazon Athena**.

4. For **Storage location**, choose the Amazon S3 bucket where log files are stored for the trail to query. **Note** You can find out what bucket is associated with a trail by going to **Trails** and choosing the trail. The bucket name is displayed in **Storage location**.

5. Choose **Create table**. The table is created with a default name that includes the name of the Amazon S3 bucket.

Manually Creating the Table for CloudTrail Logs in Athena

You can manually create tables for CloudTrail log files in the Athena console, and then run queries in Athena.

To create a table for a CloudTrail trail in the CloudTrail console

1. Copy and paste the following DDL statement into the Athena console.

2. Modify the `s3://CloudTrail_bucket_name/AWSLogs/Account_ID/` to point to the Amazon S3 bucket that contains your logs data.

3. Verify that fields are listed correctly. For more information about the full list of fields in a CloudTrail record, see CloudTrail Record Contents.

   In this example, the fields `requestParameters`, `responseElements`, and `additionalEventData` are included as part of `STRUCT` data type used in JSON. To get data out of these fields, use `JSON_EXTRACT` functions. For more information, see Extracting Data from JSON.

```
1  CREATE EXTERNAL TABLE cloudtrail_logs (
2  eventversion STRING,
3  useridentity STRUCT<
4              type:STRING,
5              principalid:STRING,
6              arn:STRING,
7              accountid:STRING,
8              invokedby:STRING,
9              accesskeyid:STRING,
10             userName:STRING,
11 sessioncontext:STRUCT<
12 attributes:STRUCT<
13             mfaauthenticated:STRING,
14             creationdate:STRING>,
15 sessionissuer:STRUCT<
16             type:STRING,
```

```
17              principalId:STRING,
18              arn:STRING,
19              accountId:STRING,
20              userName:STRING>>>,
21 eventtime STRING,
22 eventsource STRING,
23 eventname STRING,
24 awsregion STRING,
25 sourceipaddress STRING,
26 useragent STRING,
27 errorcode STRING,
28 errormessage STRING,
29 requestparameters STRING,
30 responseelements STRING,
31 additionaleventdata STRING,
32 requestid STRING,
33 eventid STRING,
34 resources ARRAY<STRUCT<
35              ARN:STRING,
36              accountId:STRING,
37              type:STRING>>,
38 eventtype STRING,
39 apiversion STRING,
40 readonly STRING,
41 recipientaccountid STRING,
42 serviceeventdetails STRING,
43 sharedeventid STRING,
44 vpcendpointid STRING
45 )
46 ROW FORMAT SERDE 'com.amazon.emr.hive.serde.CloudTrailSerde'
47 STORED AS INPUTFORMAT 'com.amazon.emr.cloudtrail.CloudTrailInputFormat'
48 OUTPUTFORMAT 'org.apache.hadoop.hive.ql.io.HiveIgnoreKeyTextOutputFormat'
49 LOCATION 's3://CloudTrail_bucket_name/AWSLogs/Account_ID/';
```

4. Run the query in the Athena console. After the query completes, Athena registers `cloudtrail_logs`, making the data in it ready for you to issue queries.

Tips for Querying CloudTrail Logs

To explore the CloudTrail logs data, use these tips:

- Before querying the logs, verify that your logs table looks the same as the one in Manually Creating the Table for CloudTrail Logs in Athena. If it is not the first table, delete the existing table using the following command: `DROP TABLE cloudtrail_logs;`.

- After you drop the existing table, re-create it. For more information, see Creating the Table for CloudTrail Logs.

  Verify that fields in your Athena query are listed correctly. For information about the full list of fields in a CloudTrail record, see CloudTrail Record Contents.

  If your query includes fields in JSON formats, such as `STRUCT`, extract data from JSON. For more information, see Extracting Data From JSON.

  Now you are ready to issue queries against your CloudTrail table.

- Start by looking at which IAM users called which API operations and from which source IP addresses.

149

- Use the following basic SQL query as your template. Paste the query to the Athena console and run it.

```
1 SELECT
2  useridentity.arn,
3  eventname,
4  sourceipaddress,
5  eventtime
6 FROM cloudtrail_logs
7 LIMIT 100;
```

- Modify the earlier query to further explore your data.

- To improve performance, include the LIMIT clause to return a specified subset of rows.

For more information, see the AWS Big Data blog post Analyze Security, Compliance, and Operational Activity Using AWS CloudTrail and Amazon Athena.

Querying Amazon CloudFront Logs

You can configure Amazon CloudFront CDN to export Web distribution access logs to Amazon Simple Storage Service. Use these logs to explore users' surfing patterns across your web properties served by CloudFront.

Before you begin querying the logs, enable Web distributions access log on your preferred CloudFront distribution. For information, see Access Logs in the *Amazon CloudFront Developer Guide*.

Make a note of the Amazon S3 bucket to which to save these logs.

Note
This procedure works for the Web distribution access logs in CloudFront. It does not apply to streaming logs from RTMP distributions.

- Creating the Table for CloudFront Logs
- Example Query for CloudFront logs

Creating the Table for CloudFront Logs

To create the CloudFront table

1. Copy and paste the following DDL statement into the Athena console. Modify the `LOCATION` for the S3 bucket that stores your logs.

   This query uses the LazySimpleSerDe by default and it is omitted.

   The column `date` is escaped using backticks (`) because it is a reserved word in Athena.

```
1  CREATE EXTERNAL TABLE IF NOT EXISTS default.cloudfront_logs (
2    `date` DATE,
3    time STRING,
4    location STRING,
5    bytes BIGINT,
6    requestip STRING,
7    method STRING,
8    host STRING,
9    uri STRING,
10   status INT,
11   referrer STRING,
12   useragent STRING,
13   querystring STRING,
14   cookie STRING,
15   resulttype STRING,
16   requestid STRING,
17   hostheader STRING,
18   requestprotocol STRING,
19   requestbytes BIGINT,
20   timetaken FLOAT,
21   xforwardedfor STRING,
22   sslprotocol STRING,
23   sslcipher STRING,
24   responseresulttype STRING,
25   httpversion STRING,
26   filestatus STRING,
27   encryptedfields INT
28 )
```

```
29 ROW FORMAT DELIMITED
30 FIELDS TERMINATED BY '\t'
31 LOCATION 's3://CloudFront_bucket_name/AWSLogs/Account_ID/'
32 TBLPROPERTIES ( 'skip.header.line.count'='2' )
```

2. Run the query in Athena console. After the query completes, Athena registers the `cloudfront_logs` table, making the data in it ready for you to issue queries.

Example Query for CloudFront logs

The following query adds up the number of bytes served by CloudFront between June 9 and June 11, 2017. Surround the date column name with double quotes because it is a reserved word.

```
1 SELECT SUM(bytes) AS total_bytes
2 FROM cloudfront_logs
3 WHERE "date" BETWEEN DATE '2017-06-09' AND DATE '2017-06-11'
4 LIMIT 100;
```

In some cases, you need to eliminate empty values from the results of `CREATE TABLE` query for CloudFront. To do so, run `SELECT DISTINCT * FROM cloudfront_logs LIMIT 10;`

For more information, see the AWS Big Data Blog post Build a Serverless Architecture to Analyze Amazon CloudFront Access Logs Using AWS Lambda, Amazon Athena, and Amazon Kinesis Analytics.

Querying Classic Load Balancer Logs

Use Classic Load Balancer logs to analyze and understand traffic patterns to and from Elastic Load Balancing instances and backend applications. You can see the source of traffic, latency, and bytes transferred.

Before you begin to analyze the Elastic Load Balancing logs, configure them for saving in the destination Amazon S3 bucket. For more information, see Enable Access Logs for Your Classic Load Balancer.

- Creating the Table for ELB Logs
- Example Queries for ELB Logs

Creating the Table for Elastic Load Balancing Logs

Create the table that you can later query. This table must include the exact location of your Elastic Load Balancing logs in Amazon S3.

To create the Elastic Load Balancing table

1. Copy and paste the following DDL statement into the Athena console.

2. Modify the `LOCATION` S3 bucket to specify the destination of your Elastic Load Balancing logs.

```
1 CREATE EXTERNAL TABLE IF NOT EXISTS elb_logs (
2   request_timestamp string,
3   elb_name string,
4   request_ip string,
5   request_port int,
6   backend_ip string,
7   backend_port int,
8   request_processing_time double,
9   backend_processing_time double,
10   client_response_time double,
11   elb_response_code string,
12   backend_response_code string,
13   received_bytes bigint,
14   sent_bytes bigint,
15   request_verb string,
16   url string,
17   protocol string,
18   user_agent string,
19   ssl_cipher string,
20   ssl_protocol string
21 )
22 ROW FORMAT SERDE 'org.apache.hadoop.hive.serde2.RegexSerDe'
23 WITH SERDEPROPERTIES (
24   'serialization.format' = '1',
25   'input.regex' = '([^ ]*) ([^ ]*) ([^ ]*):([0-9]*) ([^ ]*)[:\-]([0-9]*) ([-.0-9]*)
        ([-.0-9]*) ([-.0-9]*) (|[-0-9]*) (-|[-0-9]*) ([-0-9]*) ([-0-9]*) \\\"([^ ]*) ([^ ]*)
        (- |[^ ]*)\\\" (\"[^\"]*\") ([A-Z0-9-]+) ([A-Za-z0-9.-]*)$' )
26 LOCATION 's3://your_log_bucket/prefix/AWSLogs/AWS_account_ID/elasticloadbalancing/';
```

3. Run the query in the Athena console. After the query completes, Athena registers the `elb_logs` table, making the data in it ready for queries.

Example Queries for Elastic Load Balancing Logs

Use a query similar to this example. It lists the backend application servers that returned a **4XX** or **5XX** error response code. Use the LIMIT operator to limit the number of logs to query at a time.

```
1 SELECT
2  request_timestamp,
3  elb_name,
4  backend_ip,
5  backend_response_code
6 FROM elb_logs
7 WHERE backend_response_code LIKE '4%' OR
8        backend_response_code LIKE '5%'
9 LIMIT 100;
```

Use a subsequent query to sum up the response time of all the transactions grouped by the backend IP address and Elastic Load Balancing instance name.

```
1 SELECT sum(backend_processing_time) AS
2  total_ms,
3  elb_name,
4  backend_ip
5 FROM elb_logs WHERE backend_ip <> ''
6 GROUP BY backend_ip, elb_name
7 LIMIT 100;
```

For more information, see Analyzing Data in S3 using Athena.

Querying Application Load Balancer Logs

An Application Load Balancer is a load balancing option for Elastic Load Balancing that enables traffic distribution in a microservices deployment using containers. Querying Application Load Balancer logs allows you to see the source of traffic, latency, and bytes transferred to and from Elastic Load Balancing instances and backend applications.

Before you begin, enable access logging for Application Load Balancer logs to be saved to your Amazon S3 bucket.

- Creating the Table for ALB Logs
- Example Queries for ALB logs

Creating the Table for ALB Logs

1. Copy and paste the following DDL statement into the Athena console, and modify values in `LOCATION` `'s3://your_log_bucket/prefix/AWSLogs/your_ID/elasticloadbalancing/region'`. For a full list of fields present in the ALB logs, see Access Log Entries.

   Create the `alb_logs` table as follows:

```
1
2 CREATE EXTERNAL TABLE IF NOT EXISTS alb_logs (
3 type string,
4 time string,
5 elb string,
6 client_ip string,
7 client_port int,
8 target_ip string,
9 target_port int,
10 request_processing_time double,
11 target_processing_time double,
12 response_processing_time double,
13 elb_status_code string,
14 target_status_code string,
15 received_bytes bigint,
16 sent_bytes bigint,
17 request_verb string,
18 request_url string,
19 request_proto string,
20 user_agent string,
21 ssl_cipher string,
22 ssl_protocol string,
23 target_group_arn string,
24 trace_id string,
25 domain_name string,
26 chosen_cert_arn string,
27 matched_rule_priority string,
28 request_creation_time string,
29 actions_executed string
30 )
31 ROW FORMAT SERDE 'org.apache.hadoop.hive.serde2.RegexSerDe'
32 WITH SERDEPROPERTIES (
33 'serialization.format' = '1',
34 'input.regex' =
```

```
35 '([^ ]*) ([^ ]*) ([^ ]*) ([^ ]*):([0-9]*) ([^ ]*)[:-]([0-9]*) ([-.0-9]*) ([-.0-9]*)
     ([-.0-9]*) (|[-0-9]*) (-|[-0-9]*) ([-0-9]*) ([-0-9]*) \"([^ ]*) ([^ ]*) (- |[^ ]*)\"
     \"([^\"]*)\" ([A-Z0-9-]+) ([A-Za-z0-9.-]*) ([^ ]*) \"([^\"]*)\" \"([^\"]*)\" \"([^\"]*)
     \" ([-.0-9]*) ([^ ]*) \"([^\"]*)\"' )
36 LOCATION 's3://your-alb-logs-directory/AWSLogs/elasticloadbalancing/region';
```

2. Run the query in the Athena console. After the query completes, Athena registers the `alb_logs` table, making the data in it ready for you to issue queries.

Example Queries for ALB logs

The following query counts the number of HTTP GET requests received by the load balancer grouped by the client IP address.

```
1 SELECT COUNT(request_verb) AS
2  count,
3  request_verb,
4  client_ip
5 FROM alb_logs
6 GROUP BY request_verb, client_ip
7 LIMIT 100;
```

Another query shows the URLs visited by Safari browser users.

```
1 SELECT request_url
2 FROM alb_logs
3 WHERE user_agent LIKE '%Safari%'
4 LIMIT 10;
```

The following example shows how to parse the logs by `datetime`:

```
1 SELECT client_ip, sum(received_bytes)
2 FROM alb_logs_config_us
3 WHERE from_iso8601_date(time)
4 BETWEEN parse_datetime('2018-05-30:12:00:00','%Y-%m-%dT%H:%i:%S.%fZ')
5 AND
6 parse_datetime('2018-05-31:00:00:00','%Y-%m-%dT%H:%i:%S.%fZ')
7 GROUP BY client_ip;
```

Querying Amazon VPC Flow Logs

Amazon Virtual Private Cloud flow logs capture information about the IP traffic going to and from network interfaces in a VPC. Use the logs to investigate network traffic patterns and identify threats and risks across your VPC network.

Before you begin querying the logs in Athena, enable VPC flow logs and export log data to Amazon S3. After you create the logs, let them run for a few minutes to collect some data.

- Creating the Table for VPC Flow Logs
- Example Queries for Amazon VPC Flow Logs

Creating the Table for VPC Flow Logs

To create the Amazon VPC table

1. Copy and paste the following DDL statement into the Athena console.

2. Modify the LOCATION 's3://your_log_bucket/prefix/' to point to the S3 bucket that contains your log data.

```
1  CREATE EXTERNAL TABLE IF NOT EXISTS vpc_flow_logs (
2    ts string,
3    version int,
4    account string,
5    interfaceid string,
6    sourceaddress string,
7    destinationaddress string,
8    sourceport int,
9    destinationport int,
10   protocol int,
11   numpackets int,
12   numbytes int,
13   starttime int,
14   endtime int,
15   action string,
16   logstatus string
17 )
18 ROW FORMAT SERDE 'org.apache.hadoop.hive.serde2.RegexSerDe'
19 WITH SERDEPROPERTIES
20 ( "input.regex" = "^([^ ]+)\\s+([0-9]+)\\s+([^ ]+)\\s+([^ ]+)\\s+([^ ]+)\\s+([^ ]+)\\s
      +([0-9]+)\\s+([0-9]+)\\s+([0-9]+)\\s+([0-9]+)\\s+([0-9]+)\\s+([0-9]+)\\s+([0-9]+)\\s
      +([^ ]+)\\s+([^ ]+)$" )
21 LOCATION 's3://your_log_bucket/prefix/';
```

3. Run the query in Athena console. After the query completes, Athena registers the vpc_flow_logs table, making the data in it ready for you to issue queries.

Example Queries for Amazon VPC Flow Logs

The following query lists all of the rejected TCP connections. The query uses Date and Time Functions and Operators to convert the timestamp field ts, and extracts only the day of the week for which these events occurred.

```
1 SELECT day_of_week(from_iso8601_timestamp(ts)) AS
2   day,
3   interfaceid,
4   sourceaddress,
5   action,
6   protocol
7 FROM vpc_flow_logs
8 WHERE action = 'REJECT' AND protocol = 6
9 LIMIT 100;
```

To see which one of your servers is receiving the highest number of HTTPS requests, use this query. It counts the number of packets received on HTTPS port 443, groups them by destination IP address, and returns the top 10.

```
1 SELECT SUM(numpackets) AS
2   packetcount,
3   destinationaddress
4 FROM vpc_flow_logs
5 WHERE destinationport = 443
6 GROUP BY destinationaddress
7 ORDER BY packetcount DESC
8 LIMIT 10;
```

For more information, see the AWS Big Data blog post Analyzing VPC Flow Logs with Amazon Kinesis Firehose, Athena, and Amazon QuickSight.

Handling Schema Updates

This section provides guidance on handling schema updates for various data formats. Athena is a schema-on-read query engine. This means that when you create a table in Athena, it applies schemas when reading the data. It does not change or rewrite the underlying data.

If you anticipate changes in table schemas, consider creating them in a data format that is suitable for your needs. Your goals are to reuse existing Athena queries against evolving schemas, and avoid schema mismatch errors when querying tables with partitions.

Important
Schema updates described in this section do not work on tables with complex or nested data types, such as arrays and structs.

To achieve these goals, choose a table's data format based on the table in the following topic.

Topics

- Summary: Updates and Data Formats in Athena
- Index Access in ORC and Parquet
- Types of Updates
- Updates in Tables with Partitions

Summary: Updates and Data Formats in Athena

The following table summarizes data storage formats and their supported schema manipulations. Use this table to help you choose the format that will enable you to continue using Athena queries even as your schemas change over time.

In this table, observe that Parquet and ORC are columnar formats with different default column access methods. By default, Parquet will access columns by name and ORC by index (ordinal value). Therefore, Athena provides a SerDe property defined when creating a table to toggle the default column access method which enables greater flexibility with schema evolution.

For Parquet, the `parquet.column.index.access` property may be set to `TRUE`, which sets the column access method to use the column's ordinal number. Setting this property to `FALSE` will change the column access method to use column name. Similarly, for ORC use the `orc.column.index.access` property to control the column access method. For more information, see Index Access in ORC and Parquet.

CSV and TSV allow you to do all schema manipulations except reordering of columns, or adding columns at the beginning of the table. For example, if your schema evolution requires only renaming columns but not removing them, you can choose to create your tables in CSV or TSV. If you require removing columns, do not use CSV or TSV, and instead use any of the other supported formats, preferably, a columnar format, such as Parquet or ORC.

Schema Updates and Data Formats in Athena

Expected Type of Schema Update	Summary	CSV (with and without headers) and TSV	JSON	AVRO	PARQUET: Read by Name (default)	PARQUET: Read by Index	ORC: Read by Index (default)	ORC: Read by Name
Rename columns	Store your data in CSV and TSV, or in ORC and Parquet if they are read by index.	Y	N	N	N	Y	Y	N
Add columns at the beginning or in the middle of the table	Store your data in JSON, AVRO, or in Parquet and ORC if they are read by name. Do not use CSV and TSV.	N	Y	Y	Y	N	N	Y
Add columns at the end of the table	Store your data in CSV or TSV, JSON, AVRO, and in ORC and Parquet if they are read by name.	Y	Y	Y	Y	N	N	Y
Remove columns	Store your data in JSON, AVRO, or Parquet and ORC, if they are read by name. Do not use CSV and TSV.	N	Y	Y	Y	N	N	Y

160

Expected Type of Schema Update	Summary	CSV (with and without headers) and TSV	JSON	AVRO	PARQUET: Read by Name (default)	PARQUET: Read by Index	ORC: Read by Index (default)	ORC: Read by Name
Reorder columns	Store your data in AVRO, JSON or ORC and Parquet if they are read by name.	N	Y	Y	Y	N	N	Y
Change a column's data type	Store your data in any format, but test your query in Athena to make sure the data types are compatible.	Y	Y	Y	Y	Y	Y	Y

Index Access in ORC and Parquet

PARQUET and ORC are columnar data storage formats that can be read by index, or by name. Storing your data in either of these formats lets you perform all operations on schemas and run Athena queries without schema mismatch errors.

- Athena *reads ORC by index by default*, as defined in SERDEPROPERTIES ('orc.column.index.access'='true'). For more information, see ORC: Read by Index.
- Athena reads *Parquet by name by default*, as defined in SERDEPROPERTIES ('parquet.column.index.access'='false'). For more information, see PARQUET: Read by Name.

Since these are defaults, specifying these SerDe properties in your CREATE TABLE queries is optional, they are used implicitly. When used, they allow you to run some schema update operations while preventing other such operations. To enable those operations, run another CREATE TABLE query and change the SerDe settings.

The following sections describe these cases in detail.

ORC: Read by Index

A table in *ORC is read by index*, by default. This is defined by the following syntax:

```
1 WITH SERDEPROPERTIES (
2   'orc.column.index.access'='true')
```

Reading by index allows you to rename columns. But then you lose the ability to remove columns or add them in the middle of the table.

To make ORC read by name, which will allow you to add columns in the middle of the table or remove columns in ORC, set the SerDe property `orc.column.index.access` to FALSE in the `CREATE TABLE` statement. In this configuration, you will lose the ability to rename columns.

The following example illustrates how to change the ORC to make it read by name:

```
1  CREATE EXTERNAL TABLE orders_orc_read_by_name (
2     `o_comment` string,
3     `o_orderkey` int,
4     `o_custkey` int,
5     `o_orderpriority` string,
6     `o_orderstatus` string,
7     `o_clerk` string,
8     `o_shippriority` int,
9     `o_orderdate` string
10 )
11 ROW FORMAT SERDE
12    'org.apache.hadoop.hive.ql.io.orc.OrcSerde'
13 WITH SERDEPROPERTIES (
14    'orc.column.index.access'='false')
15 STORED AS INPUTFORMAT
16    'org.apache.hadoop.hive.ql.io.orc.OrcInputFormat'
17 OUTPUTFORMAT
18    'org.apache.hadoop.hive.ql.io.orc.OrcOutputFormat'
19 LOCATION 's3://schema_updates/orders_orc/';
```

Parquet: Read by Name

A table in *Parquet is read by name*, by default. This is defined by the following syntax:

```
1  WITH SERDEPROPERTIES (
2     'parquet.column.index.access'='false')
```

Reading by name allows you to add columns in the middle of the table and remove columns. But then you lose the ability to rename columns.

To make Parquet read by index, which will allow you to rename columns, you must create a table with `parquet.column.index.access` SerDe property set to TRUE.

Types of Updates

Here are the types of updates that a table's schema can have. We review each type of schema update and specify which data formats allow you to have them in Athena.

Important

Schema updates described in this section do not work on tables with complex or nested data types, such as arrays and structs.

- Adding Columns at the Beginning or Middle of the Table
- Adding Columns at the End of the Table
- Removing Columns
- Renaming Columns
- Reordering Columns
- Changing a Column's Data Type

Depending on how you expect your schemas to evolve, to continue using Athena queries, choose a compatible data format.

Let's consider an application that reads orders information from an `orders` table that exists in two formats: CSV and Parquet.

The following example creates a table in Parquet:

```
1  CREATE EXTERNAL TABLE orders_parquet (
2      `orderkey` int,
3      `orderstatus` string,
4      `totalprice` double,
5      `orderdate` string,
6      `orderpriority` string,
7      `clerk` string,
8      `shippriority` int
9  ) STORED AS PARQUET
10 LOCATION 's3://schema_updates/orders_ parquet/';
```

The following example creates the same table in CSV:

```
1  CREATE EXTERNAL TABLE orders_csv (
2      `orderkey` int,
3      `orderstatus` string,
4      `totalprice` double,
5      `orderdate` string,
6      `orderpriority` string,
7      `clerk` string,
8      `shippriority` int
9  )
10 ROW FORMAT DELIMITED FIELDS TERMINATED BY ','
11 LOCATION 's3://schema_updates/orders_csv/';
```

In the following sections, we review how updates to these tables affect Athena queries.

Adding Columns at the Beginning or in the Middle of the Table

Adding columns is one of the most frequent schema changes. For example, you may add a new column to enrich the table with new data. Or, you may add a new column if the source for an existing column has changed, and keep the previous version of this column, to adjust applications that depend on them.

To add columns at the beginning or in the middle of the table, and continue running queries, use AVRO, JSON, and Parquet and ORC if they are read by name. For information, see Index Access in ORC and Parquet.

Do not use CSV and TSV, as these formats depend on ordering. Adding a column at the beginning or in the middle of the table in CSV and TSV will lead to schema mismatch errors in cases when the schema of partitions changes.

The following example shows adding a column to a JSON table in the middle of the table:

```
1  CREATE EXTERNAL TABLE orders_json_column_addition (
2      `o_orderkey` int,
3      `o_custkey` int,
4      `o_orderstatus` string,
5      `o_comment` string,
6      `o_totalprice` double,
7      `o_orderdate` string,
8      `o_orderpriority` string,
9      `o_clerk` string,
10     `o_shippriority` int,
11     `o_comment` string
12 )
13 ROW FORMAT SERDE 'org.openx.data.jsonserde.JsonSerDe'
14 LOCATION 's3://schema_updates/orders_json/';
```

Adding Columns at the End of the Table

If you create tables in any of the formats that Athena supports, such as Parquet, ORC, Avro, JSON, CSV, and TSV, you can add new columns *at the end of the table*. If you use ORC formats, you must configure ORC to read by name. Parquet reads by name by default. For information, see Index Access in ORC and Parquet.

In the following example, drop an existing table in Parquet, and add a new Parquet table with a new **comment** column at the end of the table:

```
1  DROP TABLE orders_parquet;
2  CREATE EXTERNAL TABLE orders_parquet (
3      `orderkey` int,
4      `orderstatus` string,
5      `totalprice` double,
6      `orderdate` string,
7      `orderpriority` string,
8      `clerk` string,
9      `shippriority` int
10     `comment` string
11 )
12 STORED AS PARQUET
13 LOCATION 's3://schema_updates/orders_parquet/';
```

In the following example, drop an existing table in CSV and add a new CSV table with a new **comment** column at the end of the table:

```
1  DROP TABLE orders_csv;
2  CREATE EXTERNAL TABLE orders_csv (
3      `orderkey` int,
4      `orderstatus` string,
5      `totalprice` double,
6      `orderdate` string,
```

```
 7    `orderpriority` string,
 8    `clerk` string,
 9    `shippriority` int
10    `comment` string
11  )
12  ROW FORMAT DELIMITED FIELDS TERMINATED BY ','
13  LOCATION 's3://schema_updates/orders_csv/';
```

Removing Columns

You may need to remove columns from tables if they no longer contain data, or to restrict access to the data in them.

- You can remove columns from tables in JSON, Avro, and in Parquet and ORC if they are read by name. For information, see Index Access in ORC and Parquet.
- You cannot remove columns from tables in CSV and TSV.

In this example, remove a column `totalprice` from a table in Parquet and run a query. In Athena, Parquet is read by name by default, this is why we omit the SERDEPROPERTIES configuration that specifies reading by name. Notice that the following query succeeds, even though you changed the schema:

```
 1  CREATE EXTERNAL TABLE orders_parquet_column_removed (
 2    `o_orderkey` int,
 3    `o_custkey` int,
 4    `o_orderstatus` string,
 5    `o_orderdate` string,
 6    `o_orderpriority` string,
 7    `o_clerk` string,
 8    `o_shippriority` int,
 9    `o_comment` string
10  )
11  STORED AS PARQUET
12  LOCATION 's3://schema_updates/orders_parquet/';
```

Renaming Columns

You may want to rename columns in your tables to correct spelling, make column names more descriptive, or to reuse an existing column to avoid column reordering.

You can rename columns if you store your data in CSV and TSV, or in Parquet and ORC that are configured to read by index. For information, see Index Access in ORC and Parquet.

Athena reads data in CSV and TSV in the order of the columns in the schema and returns them in the same order. It does not use column names for mapping data to a column, which is why you can rename columns in CSV or TSV without breaking Athena queries.

In this example, rename the column `o_totalprice` to `o_total_price` in the Parquet table, and then run a query in Athena:

```
 1  CREATE EXTERNAL TABLE orders_parquet_column_renamed (
 2    `o_orderkey` int,
 3    `o_custkey` int,
 4    `o_orderstatus` string,
 5    `o_total_price` double,
 6    `o_orderdate` string,
```

```
7      `o_orderpriority` string,
8      `o_clerk` string,
9      `o_shippriority` int,
10     `o_comment` string
11 )
12 STORED AS PARQUET
13 LOCATION 's3://TBD/schema_updates/orders_parquet/';
```

In the Parquet table case, the following query runs, but the renamed column does not show data because the column was being accessed by name (a default in Parquet) rather than by index:

```
1 SELECT *
2 FROM orders_parquet_column_renamed;
```

A query with a table in CSV looks similar:

```
1 CREATE EXTERNAL TABLE orders_csv_column_renamed (
2      `o_orderkey` int,
3      `o_custkey` int,
4      `o_orderstatus` string,
5      `o_total_price` double,
6      `o_orderdate` string,
7      `o_orderpriority` string,
8      `o_clerk` string,
9      `o_shippriority` int,
10     `o_comment` string
11 )
12 ROW FORMAT DELIMITED FIELDS TERMINATED BY ','
13 LOCATION 's3://schema_updates/orders_csv/';
```

In the CSV table case, the following query runs and the data displays in all columns, including the one that was renamed:

```
1 SELECT *
2 FROM orders_csv_column_renamed;
```

Reordering Columns

You can reorder columns only for tables with data in formats that read by name, such as JSON or ORC, which reads by name by default. You can also make Parquet read by name, if needed. For information, see Index Access in ORC and Parquet.

The following example illustrates reordering of columns:

```
1 CREATE EXTERNAL TABLE orders_parquet_columns_reordered (
2      `o_comment` string,
3      `o_orderkey` int,
4      `o_custkey` int,
5      `o_orderpriority` string,
6      `o_orderstatus` string,
7      `o_clerk` string,
8      `o_shippriority` int,
9      `o_orderdate` string
10 )
11 STORED AS PARQUET
12 LOCATION 's3://schema_updates/orders_parquet/';
```

Changing a Column's Data Type

You change column types because a column's data type can no longer hold the amount of information, for example, when an ID column exceeds the size of an `INT` data type and has to change to a `BIGINT` data type. Only certain data types can be converted to other data types.

Note
We strongly suggest that you test and verify your queries before performing data type translations. If Athena cannot convert the data type from the original data type to the target data type, the `CREATE TABLE` query may fail.

The following table lists data types that you can change:

Compatible Data Types

Original Data Type	Available Target Data Types
STRING	BYTE, TINYINT, SMALLINT, INT, BIGINT
BYTE	TINYINT, SMALLINT, INT, BIGINT
TINYINT	SMALLINT, INT, BIGINT
SMALLINT	INT, BIGINT
INT	BIGINT
FLOAT	DOUBLE

In the following example of the `orders_json` table, change the data type for the column `o_shippriority` to `BIGINT`:

```
1 CREATE EXTERNAL TABLE orders_json (
2     `o_orderkey` int,
3     `o_custkey` int,
4     `o_orderstatus` string,
5     `o_totalprice` double,
6     `o_orderdate` string,
7     `o_orderpriority` string,
8     `o_clerk` string,
9     `o_shippriority` BIGINT
10 )
11 ROW FORMAT SERDE 'org.openx.data.jsonserde.JsonSerDe'
12 LOCATION 's3://schema_updates/orders_json';
```

The following query runs successfully, similar to the original `SELECT` query, before the data type change:

```
1 Select * from orders_json
2 LIMIT 10;
```

Updates in Tables with Partitions

In Athena, a table and its partitions must use the same data formats but their schemas may differ. When you create a new partition, that partition usually inherits the schema of the table. Over time, the schemas may start to differ. Reasons include:

- If your table's schema changes, the schemas for partitions are not updated to remain in sync with the table's schema.
- The AWS Glue Crawler allows you to discover data in partitions with different schemas. This means that if you create a table in Athena with AWS Glue, after the crawler finishes processing, the schemas for the table and its partitions may be different.
- If you add partitions directly using an AWS API.

Athena processes tables with partitions successfully if they meet the following constraints. If these constraints are not met, Athena issues a HIVE_PARTITION_SCHEMA_MISMATCH error.

- Each partition's schema is compatible with the table's schema.

- The table's data format allows the type of update you want to perform: add, delete, reorder columns, or change a column's data type.

  For example, for CSV and TSV formats, you can rename columns, add new columns at the end of the table, and change a column's data type if the types are compatible, but you cannot remove columns. For other formats, you can add or remove columns, or change a column's data type to another if the types are compatible. For information, see Summary: Updates and Data Formats in Athena.

Important
Schema updates described in this section do not work on tables with complex or nested data types, such as arrays and structs.

Avoiding Schema Mismatch Errors for Tables with Partitions

At the beginning of query execution, Athena verifies the table's schema by checking that each column data type is compatible between the table and the partition.

- For Parquet and ORC data storage types, Athena relies on the column names and uses them for its column name-based schema verification. This eliminates `HIVE_PARTITION_SCHEMA_MISMATCH` errors for tables with partitions in Parquet and ORC. (This is true for ORC if the SerDe property is set to access the index by name: `orc.column.index.access=FALSE`. Parquet reads the index by name by default).
- For CSV, JSON, and Avro, Athena uses an index-based schema verification. This means that if you encounter a schema mismatch error, you should drop the partition that is causing a schema mismatch and recreate it, so that Athena can query it without failing.

Athena compares the table's schema to the partition schemas. If you create a table in CSV, JSON, and AVRO in Athena with AWS Glue Crawler, after the Crawler finishes processing, the schemas for the table and its partitions may be different. If there is a mismatch between the table's schema and the partition schemas, your queries fail in Athena due to the schema verification error similar to this: 'crawler_test.click_avro' is declared as type 'string', but partition 'partition_0=2017-01-17' declared column 'col68' as type 'double'."

A typical workaround for such errors is to drop the partition that is causing the error and recreate it.

Monitoring Logs and Troubleshooting

Examine Athena requests using CloudTrail logs.

Topics

- Logging Amazon Athena API Calls with AWS CloudTrail
- Troubleshooting

Logging Amazon Athena API Calls with AWS CloudTrail

Athena is integrated with CloudTrail, a service that captures all of the Athena API calls and delivers the log files to an Amazon S3 bucket that you specify.

CloudTrail captures API calls from the Athena console or from your code to the Athena API operations. Using the information collected by CloudTrail, you can determine the request that was made to Athena, the source IP address from which the request was made, who made the request, when it was made, and so on.

You can also use Athena to query CloudTrail log files for insight. For more information, see CloudTrail SerDe. To learn more about CloudTrail, including how to configure and enable it, see the AWS CloudTrail User Guide.

Athena Information in CloudTrail

When CloudTrail logging is enabled in your AWS account, API calls made to Athena actions are tracked in CloudTrail log files, where they are written with other AWS service records. CloudTrail determines when to create and write to a new file based on a time period and file size.

All Athena actions are logged by CloudTrail and are documented in the Amazon Athena API Reference. For example, calls to the StartQueryExecution and GetQueryResults actions generate entries in the CloudTrail log files.

Every log entry contains information about who generated the request. The user identity information in the log entry helps you determine the following:

- Whether the request was made with root or IAM user credentials
- Whether the request was made with temporary security credentials for a role or federated user
- Whether the request was made by another AWS service

For more information, see CloudTrail userIdentity Element in the *AWS CloudTrail User Guide.*

You can store your log files in your S3 bucket for as long as you want, but you can also define Amazon S3 lifecycle rules to archive or delete log files automatically. By default, your log files are encrypted with Amazon S3 server-side encryption (SSE).

To be notified upon log file delivery, you can configure CloudTrail to publish Amazon SNS notifications when new log files are delivered. For more information, see Configuring Amazon SNS Notifications for CloudTrail.

You can also aggregate Athena log files from multiple AWS regions and multiple AWS accounts into a single S3 bucket.

For more information, see Receiving CloudTrail Log Files from Multiple Regions and Receiving CloudTrail Log Files from Multiple Accounts.

Understanding Athena Log File Entries

CloudTrail log files can contain one or more log entries. Each entry lists multiple JSON-formatted events. A log entry represents a single request from any source and includes information about the requested action, the date and time of the action, request parameters, and so on. Log entries are not an ordered stack trace of the public API calls, so they do not appear in any specific order.

The following examples demonstrate CloudTrail log entries for:

- StartQueryExecution (Successful)
- StartQueryExecution (Failed)
- CreateNamedQuery

StartQueryExecution (Successful)

```
1  {
2    "eventVersion":"1.05",
3    "userIdentity":{
4      "type":"IAMUser",
5      "principalId":"EXAMPLE_PRINCIPAL_ID",
6      "arn":"arn:aws:iam::123456789012:user/johndoe",
7      "accountId":"123456789012",
8      "accessKeyId":"EXAMPLE_KEY_ID",
9      "userName":"johndoe"
10   },
11   "eventTime":"2017-05-04T00:23:55Z",
12   "eventSource":"athena.amazonaws.com",
13   "eventName":"StartQueryExecution",
14   "awsRegion":"us-east-1",
15   "sourceIPAddress":"77.88.999.69",
16   "userAgent":"aws-internal/3",
17   "requestParameters":{
18     "clientRequestToken":"16bc6e70-f972-4260-b18a-db1b623cb35c",
19     "resultConfiguration":{
20       "outputLocation":"s3://athena-johndoe-test/test/"
21     },
22     "query":"Select 10"
23   },
24   "responseElements":{
25     "queryExecutionId":"b621c254-74e0-48e3-9630-78ed857782f9"
26   },
27   "requestID":"f5039b01-305f-11e7-b146-c3fc56a7dc7a",
28   "eventID":"c97cf8c8-6112-467a-8777-53bb38f83fd5",
29   "eventType":"AwsApiCall",
30   "recipientAccountId":"123456789012"
31 }
```

StartQueryExecution (Failed)

```
1  {
2    "eventVersion":"1.05",
3    "userIdentity":{
4     "type":"IAMUser",
5     "principalId":"EXAMPLE_PRINCIPAL_ID",
6     "arn":"arn:aws:iam::123456789012:user/johndoe",
7     "accountId":"123456789012",
8     "accessKeyId":"EXAMPLE_KEY_ID",
9     "userName":"johndoe"
10    },
11   "eventTime":"2017-05-04T00:21:57Z",
12   "eventSource":"athena.amazonaws.com",
13   "eventName":"StartQueryExecution",
14   "awsRegion":"us-east-1",
15   "sourceIPAddress":"77.88.999.69",
16   "userAgent":"aws-internal/3",
17   "errorCode":"InvalidRequestException",
18   "errorMessage":"Invalid result configuration. Should specify either output location or result
         configuration",
```

```
19    "requestParameters":{
20      "clientRequestToken":"ca0e965f-d6d8-4277-8257-814a57f57446",
21      "query":"Select 10"
22    },
23    "responseElements":null,
24    "requestID":"aefbc057-305f-11e7-9f39-bbc56d5d161e",
25    "eventID":"6e1fc69b-d076-477e-8dec-024ee51488c4",
26    "eventType":"AwsApiCall",
27    "recipientAccountId":"123456789012"
28 }
```

CreateNamedQuery

```
1  {
2    "eventVersion":"1.05",
3    "userIdentity":{
4      "type":"IAMUser",
5      "principalId":"EXAMPLE_PRINCIPAL_ID",
6      "arn":"arn:aws:iam::123456789012:user/johndoe",
7      "accountId":"123456789012",
8      "accessKeyId":"EXAMPLE_KEY_ID",
9      "userName":"johndoe"
10   },
11   "eventTime":"2017-05-16T22:00:58Z",
12   "eventSource":"athena.amazonaws.com",
13   "eventName":"CreateNamedQuery",
14   "awsRegion":"us-west-2",
15   "sourceIPAddress":"77.88.999.69",
16   "userAgent":"aws-cli/1.11.85 Python/2.7.10 Darwin/16.6.0 botocore/1.5.48",
17   "requestParameters":{
18      "name":"johndoetest",
19      "queryString":"select 10",
20      "database":"default",
21      "clientRequestToken":"fc1ad880-69ee-4df0-bb0f-1770d9a539b1"
22    },
23   "responseElements":{
24      "namedQueryId":"cdd0fe29-4787-4263-9188-a9c8db29f2d6"
25    },
26   "requestID":"2487dd96-3a83-11e7-8f67-c9de5ac76512",
27   "eventID":"15e3d3b5-6c3b-4c7c-bc0b-36a8dd95227b",
28   "eventType":"AwsApiCall",
29   "recipientAccountId":"123456789012"
30 },
```

Troubleshooting

Use these resources to troubleshoot problems with Amazon Athena.

- Service Limits
- Athena topics in the AWS Knowledge Center
- Athena discussion forum
- Athena posts in the AWS Big Data Blog

SerDe Reference

Athena supports several SerDe libraries for parsing data from different data formats, such as CSV, JSON, Parquet, and ORC. Athena does not support custom SerDes.

Topics

- Using a SerDe
- Supported SerDes and Data Formats
- Compression Formats

Using a SerDe

A SerDe (Serializer/Deserializer) is a way in which Athena interacts with data in various formats.

It is the SerDe you specify, and not the DDL, that defines the table schema. In other words, the SerDe can override the DDL configuration that you specify in Athena when you create your table.

To Use a SerDe in Queries

To use a SerDe when creating a table in Athena, use one of the following methods:

- Use DDL statements to describe how to read and write data to the table and do not specify a ROW FORMAT, as in this example. This omits listing the actual SerDe type and the native LazySimpleSerDe is used by default.

In general, Athena uses the LazySimpleSerDe if you do not specify a ROW FORMAT, or if you specify ROW FORMAT DELIMITED.

```
1 ROW FORMAT
2 DELIMITED FIELDS TERMINATED BY ','
3 ESCAPED BY '\\'
4 COLLECTION ITEMS TERMINATED BY '|'
5 MAP KEYS TERMINATED BY ':'
```

- Explicitly specify the type of SerDe Athena should use when it reads and writes data to the table. Also, specify additional properties in SERDEPROPERTIES, as in this example.

```
1 ROW FORMAT SERDE 'org.apache.hadoop.hive.serde2.lazy.LazySimpleSerDe'
2 WITH SERDEPROPERTIES (
3 'serialization.format' = ',',
4 'field.delim' = ',',
5 'collection.delim' = '|',
6 'mapkey.delim' = ':',
7 'escape.delim' = '\\'
8 )
```

Supported SerDes and Data Formats

Athena supports creating tables and querying data from files in CSV, TSV, custom-delimited, and JSON formats; files from Hadoop-related formats: ORC, Apache Avro and Parquet; log files from Logstash, AWS CloudTrail logs, and Apache WebServer logs.

To create tables and query data from files in these formats in Athena, specify a serializer-deserializer class (SerDe) so that Athena knows which format is used and how to parse the data.

This table lists the data formats supported in Athena and their corresponding SerDe libraries.

A SerDe is a custom library that tells the data catalog used by Athena how to handle the data. You specify a SerDe type by listing it explicitly in the `ROW FORMAT` part of your `CREATE TABLE` statement in Athena. In some cases, you can omit the SerDe name because Athena uses some SerDe types by default for certain types of file formats.

Supported Data Formats and SerDes

Data Format	Description	SerDe types supported in Athena
CSV (Comma-Separated Values)	In a CSV file, each line represents a data record, and each record consists of one or more fields, separated by commas.	[See the AWS documentation website for more details]
TSV (Tab-Separated Values)	In a TSV file, each line represents a data record, and each record consists of one or more fields, separated by tabs.	Use the LazySimpleSerDe for CSV, TSV, and Custom-Delimited Files and specify the separator character as `FIELDS TERMINATED BY '\t'`.
Custom-Delimited files	In a file in this format, each line represents a data record, and records are separated by custom delimiters.	Use the LazySimpleSerDe for CSV, TSV, and Custom-Delimited Files and specify custom delimiters.
JSON (JavaScript Object Notation)	In a JSON file, each line represents a data record, and each record consists of attribute–value pairs and arrays, separated by commas.	[See the AWS documentation website for more details]
Apache Avro	A format for storing data in Hadoop that uses JSON-based schemas for record values.	Use the Avro SerDe.
ORC (Optimized Row Columnar)	A format for optimized columnar storage of Hive data.	Use the ORC SerDe and ZLIB compression.
Apache Parquet	A format for columnar storage of data in Hadoop.	Use the Parquet SerDe and SNAPPY compression.
Logstash log files	A format for storing log files in Logstash.	Use the Grok SerDe.
Apache WebServer log files	A format for storing log files in Apache WebServer.	Use the RegexSerDe for Processing Apache Web Server Logs.
CloudTrail log files	A format for storing log files in CloudTrail.	[See the AWS documentation website for more details]

Topics

- Avro SerDe
- RegexSerDe for Processing Apache Web Server Logs
- CloudTrail SerDe
- OpenCSVSerDe for Processing CSV
- Grok SerDe
- JSON SerDe Libraries
- LazySimpleSerDe for CSV, TSV, and Custom-Delimited Files
- ORC SerDe
- Parquet SerDe

Avro SerDe

SerDe Name

Avro SerDe

Library Name

org.apache.hadoop.hive.serde2.avro.AvroSerDe

Examples

Athena does not support using `avro.schema.url` to specify table schema for security reasons. Use `avro.schema.literal`. To extract schema from an Avro file, you can use the Apache `avro-tools-<version>.jar` with the `getschema` parameter. This returns a schema that you can use in your `WITH SERDEPROPERTIES` statement. For example:

```
java -jar avro-tools-1.8.2.jar getschema my_data.avro
```

The `avro-tools-<version>.jar` file is located in the `java` subdirectory of your installed Avro release. To download Avro, see Apache Avro Releases. To download Apache Avro Tools directly, see the Apache Avro Tools Maven Repository.

After you obtain the schema, use a `CREATE TABLE` statement to create an Athena table based on underlying Avro data stored in Amazon S3. In `ROW FORMAT`, specify the Avro SerDe as follows: `ROW FORMAT SERDE 'org.apache.hadoop.hive.serde2.avro.AvroSerDe'` In `SERDEPROPERTIES`, specify the schema, as shown in this example.

Note
You can query data in regions other than the region where you run Athena. Standard inter-region data transfer rates for Amazon S3 apply in addition to standard Athena charges. To reduce data transfer charges, replace *myregion* in `s3://athena-examples-myregion/path/to/data/` with the region identifier where you run Athena, for example, `s3://athena-examples-us-east-1/path/to/data/`.

```
1  CREATE EXTERNAL TABLE flights_avro_example (
2      yr INT,
3      flightdate STRING,
4      uniquecarrier STRING,
5      airlineid INT,
6      carrier STRING,
7      flightnum STRING,
8      origin STRING,
9      dest STRING,
10     depdelay INT,
11     carrierdelay INT,
12     weatherdelay INT
13 )
14 PARTITIONED BY (year STRING)
15 ROW FORMAT
16 SERDE 'org.apache.hadoop.hive.serde2.avro.AvroSerDe'
17 WITH SERDEPROPERTIES ('avro.schema.literal'='
18 {
19     "type" : "record",
20     "name" : "flights_avro_subset",
```

```
21      "namespace" : "default",
22      "fields" : [ {
23        "name" : "yr",
24        "type" : [ "null", "int" ],
25        "default" : null
26      }, {
27        "name" : "flightdate",
28        "type" : [ "null", "string" ],
29        "default" : null
30      }, {
31        "name" : "uniquecarrier",
32        "type" : [ "null", "string" ],
33        "default" : null
34      }, {
35        "name" : "airlineid",
36        "type" : [ "null", "int" ],
37        "default" : null
38      }, {
39        "name" : "carrier",
40        "type" : [ "null", "string" ],
41        "default" : null
42      }, {
43        "name" : "flightnum",
44        "type" : [ "null", "string" ],
45        "default" : null
46      }, {
47        "name" : "origin",
48        "type" : [ "null", "string" ],
49        "default" : null
50      }, {
51        "name" : "dest",
52        "type" : [ "null", "string" ],
53        "default" : null
54      }, {
55        "name" : "depdelay",
56        "type" : [ "null", "int" ],
57        "default" : null
58      }, {
59        "name" : "carrierdelay",
60        "type" : [ "null", "int" ],
61        "default" : null
62      }, {
63        "name" : "weatherdelay",
64        "type" : [ "null", "int" ],
65        "default" : null
66      } ]
67 }
68 ')
69 STORED AS AVRO
70 LOCATION 's3://athena-examples-myregion/flight/avro/';
```

Run the MSCK REPAIR TABLE statement on the table to refresh partition metadata.

```
1 MSCK REPAIR TABLE flights_avro_example;
```

Query the top 10 departure cities by number of total departures.

```
1 SELECT origin, count(*) AS total_departures
2 FROM flights_avro_example
3 WHERE year >= '2000'
4 GROUP BY origin
5 ORDER BY total_departures DESC
6 LIMIT 10;
```

Note

The flight table data comes from Flights provided by US Department of Transportation, Bureau of Transportation Statistics. Desaturated from original.

RegexSerDe for Processing Apache Web Server Logs

SerDe Name

RegexSerDe

Library Name

RegexSerDe

Examples

The following example creates a table from CloudFront logs using the RegExSerDe from the Getting Started tutorial.

Note

You can query data in regions other than the region where you run Athena. Standard inter-region data transfer rates for Amazon S3 apply in addition to standard Athena charges. To reduce data transfer charges, replace *myregion* in s3://athena-examples-myregion/path/to/data/ with the region identifier where you run Athena, for example, s3://athena-examples-us-east-1/path/to/data/.

```
1  CREATE EXTERNAL TABLE IF NOT EXISTS cloudfront_logs (
2    `Date` DATE,
3    Time STRING,
4    Location STRING,
5    Bytes INT,
6    RequestIP STRING,
7    Method STRING,
8    Host STRING,
9    Uri STRING,
10   Status INT,
11   Referrer STRING,
12   os STRING,
13   Browser STRING,
14   BrowserVersion STRING
15  ) ROW FORMAT SERDE 'org.apache.hadoop.hive.serde2.RegexSerDe'
16  WITH SERDEPROPERTIES (
17  "input.regex" = "^(?!#)([^ ]+)\\s+([^ ]+)\\s+([^ ]+)\\s+([^ ]+)\\s+([^ ]+)\\s+([^ ]+)\\s+([^
        ]+)\\s+([^ ]+)\\s+([^ ]+)\\s+([^ ]+)\\s+[^\(]+[\(]([^\;]+).*\%20([^\/]+)[\/](.*)$"
18  ) LOCATION 's3://athena-examples-myregion/cloudfront/plaintext/';
```

CloudTrail SerDe

AWS CloudTrail is a service that records AWS API calls and events for AWS accounts. CloudTrail generates encrypted log files and stores them in Amazon S3. You can use Athena to query these log files directly from Amazon S3, specifying the `LOCATION` of log files.

To query CloudTrail logs in Athena, create table from the log files and use the CloudTrail SerDe to deserialize the logs data.

In addition to using the CloudTrail SerDe, instances exist where you need to use a different SerDe or to extract data from JSON. Certain fields in CloudTrail logs are STRING values that may have a variable data format, which depends on the service. As a result, the CloudTrail SerDe is unable to predictably deserialize them. To query the following fields, identify the data pattern and then use a different SerDe, such as the OpenX JSON SerDe. Alternatively, to get data out of these fields, use `JSON_EXTRACT` functions. For more information, see Extracting Data From JSON.

- `requestParameters`
- `responseElements`
- `additionalEventData`
- `serviceEventDetails`

SerDe Name

CloudTrail SerDe

Library Name

com.amazon.emr.hive.serde.CloudTrailSerde

Examples

The following example uses the CloudTrail SerDe on a fictional set of log files to create a table based on them.

In this example, the fields `requestParameters`, `responseElements`, and `additionalEventData` are included as part of STRUCT data type used in JSON. To get data out of these fields, use `JSON_EXTRACT` functions. For more information, see Extracting Data From JSON.

```
1  CREATE EXTERNAL TABLE cloudtrail_logs (
2  eventversion STRING,
3  userIdentity STRUCT<
4              type:STRING,
5              principalid:STRING,
6              arn:STRING,
7              accountid:STRING,
8              invokedby:STRING,
9              accesskeyid:STRING,
10             userName:STRING,
11 sessioncontext:STRUCT<
12 attributes:STRUCT<
13             mfaauthenticated:STRING,
14             creationdate:STRING>,
15 sessionIssuer:STRUCT<
16             type:STRING,
17             principalId:STRING,
```

```
18              arn:STRING,
19              accountId:STRING,
20              userName:STRING>>>,
21 eventTime STRING,
22 eventSource STRING,
23 eventName STRING,
24 awsRegion STRING,
25 sourceIpAddress STRING,
26 userAgent STRING,
27 errorCode STRING,
28 errorMessage STRING,
29 requestParameters STRING,
30 responseElements STRING,
31 additionalEventData STRING,
32 requestId STRING,
33 eventId STRING,
34 resources ARRAY<STRUCT<
35              ARN:STRING,
36              accountId:STRING,
37              type:STRING>>,
38 eventType STRING,
39 apiVersion STRING,
40 readOnly STRING,
41 recipientAccountId STRING,
42 serviceEventDetails STRING,
43 sharedEventID STRING,
44 vpcEndpointId STRING
45 )
46 ROW FORMAT SERDE 'com.amazon.emr.hive.serde.CloudTrailSerde'
47 STORED AS INPUTFORMAT 'com.amazon.emr.cloudtrail.CloudTrailInputFormat'
48 OUTPUTFORMAT 'org.apache.hadoop.hive.ql.io.HiveIgnoreKeyTextOutputFormat'
49 LOCATION 's3://cloudtrail_bucket_name/AWSLogs/Account_ID/';
```

The following query returns the logins that occurred over a 24-hour period.

```
1 SELECT
2  useridentity.username,
3  sourceipaddress,
4  eventtime,
5  additionaleventdata
6 FROM default.cloudtrail_logs
7 WHERE eventname = 'ConsoleLogin'
8      AND eventtime >= '2017-02-17T00:00:00Z'
9      AND eventtime < '2017-02-18T00:00:00Z';
```

For more information, see Querying AWS CloudTrail Logs.

OpenCSVSerDe for Processing CSV

When you create a table from a CSV file in Athena, determine what types of values it contains:

- If the file contains values enclosed in quotes, use the OpenCSV SerDe to deserialize the values in Athena.
- If the file does not contain values enclosed in quotes, you can omit specifying any SerDe. In this case, Athena uses the default `LazySimpleSerDe`. For information, see LazySimpleSerDe for CSV, TSV, and Custom-Delimited Files.

CSV SerDe (OpenCSVSerde)

The OpenCSV SerDe behaves as follows:

- Allows you to specify separator, quote, and escape characters, such as: `WITH SERDEPROPERTIES ("separatorChar" = ",", "quoteChar" = "", "escapeChar" = "\" )`
- Does not support embedded line breaks in CSV files.
- Converts all column type values to `STRING`.
- To recognize data types other than `STRING`, relies on the Presto parser and converts the values from `STRING` into those data types if it can recognize them.

In particular, for data types other than `STRING` this SerDe behaves as follows:

- Recognizes `BOOLEAN`, `BIGINT`, `INT`, and `DOUBLE` data types and parses them without changes.
- Recognizes the `TIMESTAMP` type if it is specified in the UNIX format, such as `yyyy-mm-dd hh:mm:ss[.f...]`, as the type `LONG`.
- Does not support `TIMESTAMP` in the JDBC-compliant `java.sql.Timestamp` format, such as `"YYYY-MM-DD HH:MM:SS.fffffffff"` (9 decimal place precision). If you are processing CSV files from Hive, use the UNIX format for `TIMESTAMP`.
- Recognizes the `DATE` type if it is specified in the UNIX format, such as `YYYY-MM-DD`, as the type `LONG`.
- Does not support `DATE` in another format. If you are processing CSV files from Hive, use the UNIX format for `DATE`.

SerDe Name

CSV SerDe

Library Name

To use this SerDe, specify its fully qualified class name in `ROW FORMAT`, also specify the delimiters inside `SERDEPROPERTIES`, as follows:

```
...
ROW FORMAT SERDE 'org.apache.hadoop.hive.serde2.OpenCSVSerde'
WITH SERDEPROPERTIES (
  "separatorChar" = ",",
  "quoteChar"     = "`",
  "escapeChar"    = "\\"
)
```

Example

This example presumes a source CSV file saved in `s3://mybucket/mycsv/` with the following data contents:

```
1  "a1","a2","a3","a4"
2  "1","2","abc","def"
3  "a","a1","abc3","ab4"
```

Use a **CREATE TABLE** statement to create an Athena table based on this CSV file and reference the OpenCSVSerDe class in `ROW FORMAT`, also specifying SerDe properties for character separator, quote character, and escape character.

```
1  CREATE EXTERNAL TABLE myopencsvtable (
2      col1 string,
3      col2 string,
4      col3 string,
5      col4 string
6  )
7  ROW FORMAT SERDE 'org.apache.hadoop.hive.serde2.OpenCSVSerde'
8  WITH SERDEPROPERTIES (
9      'separatorChar' = ',',
10     'quoteChar' = '\"',
11     'escapeChar' = '\\'
12     )
13 STORED AS TEXTFILE
14 LOCATION 's3://location/of/csv/';
```

Query all values in the table.

```
1  SELECT * FROM myopencsvtable;
```

The query returns the following values.

```
1  col1        col2        col3        col4
2  ----------------------------------------
3  a1          a2          a3          a4
4  1           2           abc         def
5  a           a1          abc3        ab4
```

Note
The flight table data comes from Flights provided by US Department of Transportation, Bureau of Transportation Statistics. Desaturated from original.

Grok SerDe

The Logstash Grok SerDe is a library with a set of specialized patterns for deserialization of unstructured text files, usually logs. Each Grok pattern is a named regular expression. You can identify and re-use these deserialization patterns as needed. This makes it easier to use Grok compared with using regular expressions. Grok provides a set of pre-defined patterns. You can also create custom patterns.

To specify the Grok SerDe when creating a table in Athena, use the ROW FORMAT SERDE 'com.amazonaws.glue .serde.GrokSerDe' clause, followed by the WITH SERDEPROPERTIES clause that specifies the patterns to match in your data, where:

- The input.format expression defines the patterns to match in the data file. It is required.
- The input.grokCustomPatterns expression defines a named custom pattern, which you can subsequently use within the input.format expression. It is optional.
- The STORED AS INPUTFORMAT and OUTPUTFORMAT clauses are required.
- The LOCATION clause specifies an Amazon S3 bucket, which can contain multiple source data files. All files in the bucket are deserialized to create the table.

Examples

These examples rely on the list of predefined Grok patterns. See pre-defined patterns.

Example 1

This example uses a single fictional text file saved in s3://mybucket/groksample with the following data, which represents Postfix maillog entries.

```
1 Feb  9 07:15:00 m4eastmail postfix/smtpd[19305]: B88C4120838: connect from unknown[192.168.55.4]
2 Feb  9 07:15:00 m4eastmail postfix/smtpd[20444]: B58C4330038: client=unknown[192.168.55.4]
3 Feb  9 07:15:03 m4eastmail postfix/cleanup[22835]: BDC22A77854: message-id
      =<31221401257553.5004389LCBF@m4eastmail.example.com>
```

The following statement creates a table in Athena called mygroktable from the source data file, using a custom pattern and the predefined patterns that you specify.

```
1 CREATE EXTERNAL TABLE `mygroktable`(
2    syslogbase string,
3    queue_id string,
4    syslog_message string
5    )
6 ROW FORMAT SERDE
7    'com.amazonaws.glue.serde.GrokSerDe'
8 WITH SERDEPROPERTIES (
9    'input.grokCustomPatterns' = 'POSTFIX_QUEUEID [0-9A-F]{7,12}',
10   'input.format'='%{SYSLOGBASE} %{POSTFIX_QUEUEID:queue_id}: %{GREEDYDATA:syslog_message}'
11   )
12 STORED AS INPUTFORMAT
13   'org.apache.hadoop.mapred.TextInputFormat'
14 OUTPUTFORMAT
15   'org.apache.hadoop.hive.ql.io.HiveIgnoreKeyTextOutputFormat'
16 LOCATION
17   's3://mybucket/groksample';
```

Start with a simple pattern, such as %{NOTSPACE:column}, to get the columns mapped first and then specialize the columns if you want to.

Example 2

In the following example, you create a query for Log4j logs. The example log file has the entries in this format:

```
1 2017-09-12 12:10:34,972 INFO  - processType=AZ, processId=ABCDEFG614B6F5E49, status=RUN,
2 threadId=123:amqListenerContainerPool23[P:AJ|ABCDE9614B6F5E49||2017-09-12T12:10:11.172-0700],
3 executionTime=7290, tenantId=12456, userId=123123f8535f8d76015374e7a1d87c3c, shard=testapp1,
4 jobId=12312345e5e7df0015e777fb2e03f3c, messageType=REAL_TIME_SYNC,
5 action=receive, hostname=1.abc.def.com
```

To query this log file:

- Add the Grok pattern to the `input.format` for each column. For example, for `timestamp`, add `%{TIMESTAMP_ISO8601:timestamp}`. For `loglevel`, add `%{LOGLEVEL:loglevel}`.

- Make sure the pattern in `input.format` matches the format of the log exactly, by mapping the dashes (-) and the commas that separate the entries in the log format.

```
1  CREATE EXTERNAL TABLE bltest (
2   timestamp STRING,
3   loglevel STRING,
4   processtype STRING,
5   processid STRING,
6   status STRING,
7   threadid STRING,
8   executiontime INT,
9   tenantid INT,
10  userid STRING,
11  shard STRING,
12  jobid STRING,
13  messagetype STRING,
14  action STRING,
15  hostname STRING
16  )
17 ROW FORMAT SERDE 'com.amazonaws.glue.serde.GrokSerDe'
18 WITH SERDEPROPERTIES (
19 "input.grokCustomPatterns" = 'C_ACTION receive|send',
20 "input.format" = "%{TIMESTAMP_ISO8601:timestamp}, %{LOGLEVEL:loglevel} - processType=%{
       NOTSPACE:processtype}, processId=%{NOTSPACE:processid}, status=%{NOTSPACE:status},
       threadId=%{NOTSPACE:threadid}, executionTime=%{POSINT:executiontime}, tenantId=%{POSINT
       :tenantid}, userId=%{NOTSPACE:userid}, shard=%{NOTSPACE:shard}, jobId=%{NOTSPACE:jobid
       }, messageType=%{NOTSPACE:messagetype}, action=%{C_ACTION:action}, hostname=%{HOST:
       hostname}"
21 ) STORED AS INPUTFORMAT 'org.apache.hadoop.mapred.TextInputFormat'
22 OUTPUTFORMAT 'org.apache.hadoop.hive.ql.io.HiveIgnoreKeyTextOutputFormat'
23 LOCATION 's3://mybucket/samples/';
```

JSON SerDe Libraries

In Athena, you can use two SerDe libraries for processing JSON files:

- The native Hive JSON SerDe
- The OpenX JSON SerDe

SerDe Names

Hive-JsonSerDe

Openx-JsonSerDe

Library Names

Use one of the following:

org.apache.hive.hcatalog.data.JsonSerDe

org.openx.data.jsonserde.JsonSerDe

Hive JSON SerDe

The Hive JSON SerDe is used to process JSON documents, most commonly events. These events are represented as blocks of JSON-encoded text separated by a new line.

You can also use the Hive JSON SerDe to parse more complex JSON documents with nested structures. However, this requires having a matching DDL representing the complex data types. See Example: Deserializing Nested JSON.

This SerDe has a useful property you can specify when creating tables in Athena, to help deal with inconsistencies in the data:

- `'ignore.malformed.json'` if set to `TRUE`, lets you skip malformed JSON syntax.

Note
You can query data in regions other than the region where you run Athena. Standard inter-region data transfer rates for Amazon S3 apply in addition to standard Athena charges. To reduce data transfer charges, replace *myregion* in `s3://athena-examples-myregion/path/to/data/` with the region identifier where you run Athena, for example, `s3://athena-examples-us-east-1/path/to/data/`.

The following DDL statement uses the Hive JSON SerDe:

```
1  CREATE EXTERNAL TABLE impressions (
2      requestbegintime string,
3      adid string,
4      impressionid string,
5      referrer string,
6      useragent string,
7      usercookie string,
8      ip string,
9      number string,
10     processid string,
11     browsercookie string,
12     requestendtime string,
13     timers struct
```

```
14                   <
15                       modellookup:string,
16                       requesttime:string
17                   >,
18       threadid string,
19       hostname string,
20       sessionid string
21  )
22  PARTITIONED BY (dt string)
23  ROW FORMAT  serde 'org.apache.hive.hcatalog.data.JsonSerDe'
24  with serdeproperties ( 'paths'='requestbegintime, adid, impressionid, referrer, useragent,
        usercookie, ip' )
25  LOCATION 's3://myregion.elasticmapreduce/samples/hive-ads/tables/impressions';
```

OpenX JSON SerDe

The following DDL statement uses the OpenX JSON SerDe:

```
1   CREATE EXTERNAL TABLE impressions (
2       requestbegintime string,
3       adid string,
4       impressionId string,
5       referrer string,
6       useragent string,
7       usercookie string,
8       ip string,
9       number string,
10      processid string,
11      browsercokie string,
12      requestendtime string,
13      timers struct<
14          modellookup:string,
15          requesttime:string>,
16      threadid string,
17      hostname string,
18      sessionid string
19  )   PARTITIONED BY (dt string)
20  ROW FORMAT  serde 'org.openx.data.jsonserde.JsonSerDe'
21  with serdeproperties ( 'paths'='requestbegintime, adid, impressionid, referrer, useragent,
        usercookie, ip' )
22  LOCATION 's3://myregion.elasticmapreduce/samples/hive-ads/tables/impressions';
```

Example: Deserializing Nested JSON

JSON data can be challenging to deserialize when creating a table in Athena.

When dealing with complex nested JSON, there are common issues you may encounter. For more information about these issues and troubleshooting practices, see the AWS Knowledge Center Article I receive errors when I try to read JSON data in Amazon Athena.

For more information about common scenarios and query tips, see Create Tables in Amazon Athena from Nested JSON and Mappings Using JSONSerDe.

The following example demonstrates a simple approach to creating an Athena table from a nested JSON file. To parse JSON-encoded files in Athena, each JSON document must be on its own line, separated by a new line.

This example presumes a JSON file with the following structure:

```
{
"DocId": "AWS",
"User": {
        "Id": 1234,
        "Username": "bob1234",
        "Name": "Bob",
"ShippingAddress": {
"Address1": "123 Main St.",
"Address2": null,
"City": "Seattle",
"State": "WA"
    },
"Orders": [
    {
      "ItemId": 6789,
      "OrderDate": "11/11/2017"
    },
    {
      "ItemId": 4352,
      "OrderDate": "12/12/2017"
    }
  ]
 }
}
```

The following **CREATE TABLE** command uses the Openx-JsonSerDe with collection data types like **struct** and **array** to establish groups of objects. Each JSON document is on its own line, separated by a new line.

```
CREATE external TABLE complex_json (
    docid string,
    `user` struct<
                id:INT,
                username:string,
                name:string,
                shippingaddress:struct<
                                    address1:string,
                                    address2:string,
                                    city:string,
                                    state:string
                                    >,
                orders:array<
                            struct<
                                itemid:INT,
                                orderdate:string
                                >
                        >
            >
    )
ROW FORMAT SERDE 'org.openx.data.jsonserde.JsonSerDe'
LOCATION 's3://mybucket/myjsondata/';
```

LazySimpleSerDe for CSV, TSV, and Custom-Delimited Files

Specifying this SerDe is optional. This is the SerDe for files in CSV, TSV, and custom-delimited formats that Athena uses by default. This SerDe is used if you don't specify any SerDe and only specify `ROW FORMAT DELIMITED`. Use this SerDe if your data does not have values enclosed in quotes.

Library Name

The Class library name for the LazySimpleSerDe is `org.apache.hadoop.hive.serde2.lazy.LazySimpleSerDe`. For more information, see LazySimpleSerDe

Examples

The following examples show how to create tables in Athena from CSV and TSV, using the `LazySimpleSerDe`. To deserialize custom-delimited file using this SerDe, specify the delimiters similar to the following examples.

- CSV Example
- TSV Example

Note
You can query data in regions other than the region where you run Athena. Standard inter-region data transfer rates for Amazon S3 apply in addition to standard Athena charges. To reduce data transfer charges, replace *myregion* in `s3://athena-examples-myregion/path/to/data/` with the region identifier where you run Athena, for example, `s3://athena-examples-us-east-1/path/to/data/`.

Note
The flight table data comes from Flights provided by US Department of Transportation, Bureau of Transportation Statistics. Desaturated from original.

CSV Example

Use the `CREATE TABLE` statement to create an Athena table from the underlying CSV file stored in Amazon S3.

```
1  CREATE EXTERNAL TABLE flight_delays_csv (
2      yr INT,
3      quarter INT,
4      month INT,
5      dayofmonth INT,
6      dayofweek INT,
7      flightdate STRING,
8      uniquecarrier STRING,
9      airlineid INT,
10     carrier STRING,
11     tailnum STRING,
12     flightnum STRING,
13     originairportid INT,
14     originairportseqid INT,
15     origincitymarketid INT,
16     origin STRING,
17     origincityname STRING,
18     originstate STRING,
19     originstatefips STRING,
20     originstatename STRING,
```

```
21    originwac INT,
22    destairportid INT,
23    destairportseqid INT,
24    destcitymarketid INT,
25    dest STRING,
26    destcityname STRING,
27    deststate STRING,
28    deststatefips STRING,
29    deststatename STRING,
30    destwac INT,
31    crsdeptime STRING,
32    deptime STRING,
33    depdelay INT,
34    depdelayminutes INT,
35    depdel15 INT,
36    departuredelaygroups INT,
37    deptimeblk STRING,
38    taxiout INT,
39    wheelsoff STRING,
40    wheelson STRING,
41    taxiin INT,
42    crsarrtime INT,
43    arrtime STRING,
44    arrdelay INT,
45    arrdelayminutes INT,
46    arrdel15 INT,
47    arrivaldelaygroups INT,
48    arrtimeblk STRING,
49    cancelled INT,
50    cancellationcode STRING,
51    diverted INT,
52    crselapsedtime INT,
53    actualelapsedtime INT,
54    airtime INT,
55    flights INT,
56    distance INT,
57    distancegroup INT,
58    carrierdelay INT,
59    weatherdelay INT,
60    nasdelay INT,
61    securitydelay INT,
62    lateaircraftdelay INT,
63    firstdeptime STRING,
64    totaladdgtime INT,
65    longestaddgtime INT,
66    divairportlandings INT,
67    divreacheddest INT,
68    divactualelapsedtime INT,
69    divarrdelay INT,
70    divdistance INT,
71    div1airport STRING,
72    div1airportid INT,
73    div1airportseqid INT,
74    div1wheelson STRING,
```

```
 75      div1totalgtime INT,
 76      div1longestgtime INT,
 77      div1wheelsoff STRING,
 78      div1tailnum STRING,
 79      div2airport STRING,
 80      div2airportid INT,
 81      div2airportseqid INT,
 82      div2wheelson STRING,
 83      div2totalgtime INT,
 84      div2longestgtime INT,
 85      div2wheelsoff STRING,
 86      div2tailnum STRING,
 87      div3airport STRING,
 88      div3airportid INT,
 89      div3airportseqid INT,
 90      div3wheelson STRING,
 91      div3totalgtime INT,
 92      div3longestgtime INT,
 93      div3wheelsoff STRING,
 94      div3tailnum STRING,
 95      div4airport STRING,
 96      div4airportid INT,
 97      div4airportseqid INT,
 98      div4wheelson STRING,
 99      div4totalgtime INT,
100      div4longestgtime INT,
101      div4wheelsoff STRING,
102      div4tailnum STRING,
103      div5airport STRING,
104      div5airportid INT,
105      div5airportseqid INT,
106      div5wheelson STRING,
107      div5totalgtime INT,
108      div5longestgtime INT,
109      div5wheelsoff STRING,
110      div5tailnum STRING
111  )
112      PARTITIONED BY (year STRING)
113      ROW FORMAT DELIMITED
114        FIELDS TERMINATED BY ','
115        ESCAPED BY '\\'
116        LINES TERMINATED BY '\n'
117      LOCATION 's3://athena-examples-myregion/flight/csv/';
```

Run MSCK REPAIR TABLE to refresh partition metadata each time a new partition is added to this table.

```
1 MSCK REPAIR TABLE flight_delays_csv;
```

Query the top 10 routes delayed by more than 1 hour.

```
1 SELECT origin, dest, count(*) as delays
2 FROM flight_delays_csv
3 WHERE depdelayminutes > 60
4 GROUP BY origin, dest
5 ORDER BY 3 DESC
6 LIMIT 10;
```

TSV Example

This example presumes a source TSV file saved in `s3://mybucket/mytsv/`.

Use a `CREATE TABLE` statement to create an Athena table from the TSV file stored in Amazon S3. Notice that this example does not reference any SerDe class in `ROW FORMAT` because it uses the LazySimpleSerDe, and it can be omitted. The example specifies SerDe properties for character and line separators, and an escape character:

```
1  CREATE EXTERNAL TABLE flight_delays_tsv (
2    yr INT,
3    quarter INT,
4    month INT,
5    dayofmonth INT,
6    dayofweek INT,
7    flightdate STRING,
8    uniquecarrier STRING,
9    airlineid INT,
10   carrier STRING,
11   tailnum STRING,
12   flightnum STRING,
13   originairportid INT,
14   originairportseqid INT,
15   origincitymarketid INT,
16   origin STRING,
17   origincityname STRING,
18   originstate STRING,
19   originstatefips STRING,
20   originstatename STRING,
21   originwac INT,
22   destairportid INT,
23   destairportseqid INT,
24   destcitymarketid INT,
25   dest STRING,
26   destcityname STRING,
27   deststate STRING,
28   deststatefips STRING,
29   deststatename STRING,
30   destwac INT,
31   crsdeptime STRING,
32   deptime STRING,
33   depdelay INT,
34   depdelayminutes INT,
35   depdel15 INT,
36   departuredelaygroups INT,
37   deptimeblk STRING,
38   taxiout INT,
39   wheelsoff STRING,
40   wheelson STRING,
41   taxiin INT,
42   crsarrtime INT,
43   arrtime STRING,
44   arrdelay INT,
45   arrdelayminutes INT,
46   arrdel15 INT,
47   arrivaldelaygroups INT,
48   arrtimeblk STRING,
```

```
49  cancelled INT,
50  cancellationcode STRING,
51  diverted INT,
52  crselapsedtime INT,
53  actualelapsedtime INT,
54  airtime INT,
55  flights INT,
56  distance INT,
57  distancegroup INT,
58  carrierdelay INT,
59  weatherdelay INT,
60  nasdelay INT,
61  securitydelay INT,
62  lateaircraftdelay INT,
63  firstdeptime STRING,
64  totaladdgtime INT,
65  longestaddgtime INT,
66  divairportlandings INT,
67  divreacheddest INT,
68  divactualelapsedtime INT,
69  divarrdelay INT,
70  divdistance INT,
71  div1airport STRING,
72  div1airportid INT,
73  div1airportseqid INT,
74  div1wheelson STRING,
75  div1totalgtime INT,
76  div1longestgtime INT,
77  div1wheelsoff STRING,
78  div1tailnum STRING,
79  div2airport STRING,
80  div2airportid INT,
81  div2airportseqid INT,
82  div2wheelson STRING,
83  div2totalgtime INT,
84  div2longestgtime INT,
85  div2wheelsoff STRING,
86  div2tailnum STRING,
87  div3airport STRING,
88  div3airportid INT,
89  div3airportseqid INT,
90  div3wheelson STRING,
91  div3totalgtime INT,
92  div3longestgtime INT,
93  div3wheelsoff STRING,
94  div3tailnum STRING,
95  div4airport STRING,
96  div4airportid INT,
97  div4airportseqid INT,
98  div4wheelson STRING,
99  div4totalgtime INT,
100 div4longestgtime INT,
101 div4wheelsoff STRING,
102 div4tailnum STRING,
```

```
103  div5airport STRING,
104  div5airportid INT,
105  div5airportseqid INT,
106  div5wheelson STRING,
107  div5totalgtime INT,
108  div5longestgtime INT,
109  div5wheelsoff STRING,
110  div5tailnum STRING
111  )
112  PARTITIONED BY (year STRING)
113  ROW FORMAT DELIMITED
114    FIELDS TERMINATED BY '\t'
115    ESCAPED BY '\\'
116    LINES TERMINATED BY '\n'
117  LOCATION 's3://athena-examples-myregion/flight/tsv/';
```

Run MSCK REPAIR TABLE to refresh partition metadata each time a new partition is added to this table.

```
1  MSCK REPAIR TABLE flight_delays_tsv;
```

Query the top 10 routes delayed by more than 1 hour.

```
1  SELECT origin, dest, count(*) as delays
2  FROM flight_delays_tsv
3  WHERE depdelayminutes > 60
4  GROUP BY origin, dest
5  ORDER BY 3 DESC
6  LIMIT 10;
```

Note

The flight table data comes from Flights provided by US Department of Transportation, Bureau of Transportation Statistics. Desaturated from original.

ORC SerDe

SerDe Name

OrcSerDe

Library Name

This is the SerDe class for ORC files. It passes the object from the ORC file to the reader and from the ORC file to the writer: OrcSerDe

Examples

Note

You can query data in regions other than the region where you run Athena. Standard inter-region data transfer rates for Amazon S3 apply in addition to standard Athena charges. To reduce data transfer charges, replace *myregion* in s3://athena-examples-myregion/path/to/data/ with the region identifier where you run Athena, for example, s3://athena-examples-us-east-1/path/to/data/.

The following example creates a table for the flight delays data in ORC. The table includes partitions:

```
1  DROP TABLE flight_delays_orc;
2  CREATE EXTERNAL TABLE flight_delays_orc (
3      yr INT,
4      quarter INT,
5      month INT,
6      dayofmonth INT,
7      dayofweek INT,
8      flightdate STRING,
9      uniquecarrier STRING,
10     airlineid INT,
11     carrier STRING,
12     tailnum STRING,
13     flightnum STRING,
14     originairportid INT,
15     originairportseqid INT,
16     origincitymarketid INT,
17     origin STRING,
18     origincityname STRING,
19     originstate STRING,
20     originstatefips STRING,
21     originstatename STRING,
22     originwac INT,
23     destairportid INT,
24     destairportseqid INT,
25     destcitymarketid INT,
26     dest STRING,
27     destcityname STRING,
28     deststate STRING,
29     deststatefips STRING,
30     deststatename STRING,
31     destwac INT,
32     crsdeptime STRING,
```

```
33    deptime STRING,
34    depdelay INT,
35    depdelayminutes INT,
36    depdel15 INT,
37    departuredelaygroups INT,
38    deptimeblk STRING,
39    taxiout INT,
40    wheelsoff STRING,
41    wheelson STRING,
42    taxiin INT,
43    crsarrtime INT,
44    arrtime STRING,
45    arrdelay INT,
46    arrdelayminutes INT,
47    arrdel15 INT,
48    arrivaldelaygroups INT,
49    arrtimeblk STRING,
50    cancelled INT,
51    cancellationcode STRING,
52    diverted INT,
53    crselapsedtime INT,
54    actualelapsedtime INT,
55    airtime INT,
56    flights INT,
57    distance INT,
58    distancegroup INT,
59    carrierdelay INT,
60    weatherdelay INT,
61    nasdelay INT,
62    securitydelay INT,
63    lateaircraftdelay INT,
64    firstdeptime STRING,
65    totaladdgtime INT,
66    longestaddgtime INT,
67    divairportlandings INT,
68    divreacheddest INT,
69    divactualelapsedtime INT,
70    divarrdelay INT,
71    divdistance INT,
72    div1airport STRING,
73    div1airportid INT,
74    div1airportseqid INT,
75    div1wheelson STRING,
76    div1totalgtime INT,
77    div1longestgtime INT,
78    div1wheelsoff STRING,
79    div1tailnum STRING,
80    div2airport STRING,
81    div2airportid INT,
82    div2airportseqid INT,
83    div2wheelson STRING,
84    div2totalgtime INT,
85    div2longestgtime INT,
86    div2wheelsoff STRING,
```

```
 87      div2tailnum STRING,
 88      div3airport STRING,
 89      div3airportid INT,
 90      div3airportseqid INT,
 91      div3wheelson STRING,
 92      div3totalgtime INT,
 93      div3longestgtime INT,
 94      div3wheelsoff STRING,
 95      div3tailnum STRING,
 96      div4airport STRING,
 97      div4airportid INT,
 98      div4airportseqid INT,
 99      div4wheelson STRING,
100      div4totalgtime INT,
101      div4longestgtime INT,
102      div4wheelsoff STRING,
103      div4tailnum STRING,
104      div5airport STRING,
105      div5airportid INT,
106      div5airportseqid INT,
107      div5wheelson STRING,
108      div5totalgtime INT,
109      div5longestgtime INT,
110      div5wheelsoff STRING,
111      div5tailnum STRING
112  )
113  PARTITIONED BY (year String)
114  STORED AS ORC
115  LOCATION 's3://athena-examples-myregion/flight/orc/'
116  tblproperties ("orc.compress"="ZLIB");
```

Run the `MSCK REPAIR TABLE` statement on the table to refresh partition metadata.

```
  1  MSCK REPAIR TABLE flight_delays_orc;
```

Use this query to obtain the top 10 routes delayed by more than 1 hour:

```
  1  SELECT origin, dest, count(*) as delays
  2  FROM flight_delays_pq
  3  WHERE depdelayminutes > 60
  4  GROUP BY origin, dest
  5  ORDER BY 3 DESC
  6  LIMIT 10;
```

Parquet SerDe

SerDe Name

ParquetHiveSerDe is used for files stored in Parquet. For more information, see Parquet Format.

Library Name

Athena uses this class when it needs to deserialize files stored in Parquet: org.apache.hadoop.hive.ql.io.parquet.serde.ParquetHiveSerDe

Example: Querying a File Stored in Parquet

Note

You can query data in regions other than the region where you run Athena. Standard inter-region data transfer rates for Amazon S3 apply in addition to standard Athena charges. To reduce data transfer charges, replace *myregion* in `s3://athena-examples-myregion/path/to/data/` with the region identifier where you run Athena, for example, `s3://athena-examples-us-east-1/path/to/data/`.

Use the `CREATE TABLE` statement to create an Athena table from the underlying CSV file stored in Amazon S3 in Parquet.

```
1 CREATE EXTERNAL TABLE flight_delays_pq (
2     yr INT,
3     quarter INT,
4     month INT,
5     dayofmonth INT,
6     dayofweek INT,
7     flightdate STRING,
8     uniquecarrier STRING,
9     airlineid INT,
10     carrier STRING,
11     tailnum STRING,
12     flightnum STRING,
13     originairportid INT,
14     originairportseqid INT,
15     origincitymarketid INT,
16     origin STRING,
17     origincityname STRING,
18     originstate STRING,
19     originstatefips STRING,
20     originstatename STRING,
21     originwac INT,
22     destairportid INT,
23     destairportseqid INT,
24     destcitymarketid INT,
25     dest STRING,
26     destcityname STRING,
27     deststate STRING,
28     deststatefips STRING,
29     deststatename STRING,
30     destwac INT,
31     crsdeptime STRING,
```

199

```
32    deptime STRING,
33    depdelay INT,
34    depdelayminutes INT,
35    depdel15 INT,
36    departuredelaygroups INT,
37    deptimeblk STRING,
38    taxiout INT,
39    wheelsoff STRING,
40    wheelson STRING,
41    taxiin INT,
42    crsarrtime INT,
43    arrtime STRING,
44    arrdelay INT,
45    arrdelayminutes INT,
46    arrdel15 INT,
47    arrivaldelaygroups INT,
48    arrtimeblk STRING,
49    cancelled INT,
50    cancellationcode STRING,
51    diverted INT,
52    crselapsedtime INT,
53    actualelapsedtime INT,
54    airtime INT,
55    flights INT,
56    distance INT,
57    distancegroup INT,
58    carrierdelay INT,
59    weatherdelay INT,
60    nasdelay INT,
61    securitydelay INT,
62    lateaircraftdelay INT,
63    firstdeptime STRING,
64    totaladdgtime INT,
65    longestaddgtime INT,
66    divairportlandings INT,
67    divreacheddest INT,
68    divactualelapsedtime INT,
69    divarrdelay INT,
70    divdistance INT,
71    div1airport STRING,
72    div1airportid INT,
73    div1airportseqid INT,
74    div1wheelson STRING,
75    div1totalgtime INT,
76    div1longestgtime INT,
77    div1wheelsoff STRING,
78    div1tailnum STRING,
79    div2airport STRING,
80    div2airportid INT,
81    div2airportseqid INT,
82    div2wheelson STRING,
83    div2totalgtime INT,
84    div2longestgtime INT,
85    div2wheelsoff STRING,
```

```
86      div2tailnum STRING,
87      div3airport STRING,
88      div3airportid INT,
89      div3airportseqid INT,
90      div3wheelson STRING,
91      div3totalgtime INT,
92      div3longestgtime INT,
93      div3wheelsoff STRING,
94      div3tailnum STRING,
95      div4airport STRING,
96      div4airportid INT,
97      div4airportseqid INT,
98      div4wheelson STRING,
99      div4totalgtime INT,
100     div4longestgtime INT,
101     div4wheelsoff STRING,
102     div4tailnum STRING,
103     div5airport STRING,
104     div5airportid INT,
105     div5airportseqid INT,
106     div5wheelson STRING,
107     div5totalgtime INT,
108     div5longestgtime INT,
109     div5wheelsoff STRING,
110     div5tailnum STRING
111 )
112 PARTITIONED BY (year STRING)
113 STORED AS PARQUET
114 LOCATION 's3://athena-examples-myregion/flight/parquet/'
115 tblproperties ("parquet.compress"="SNAPPY");
```

Run the MSCK REPAIR TABLE statement on the table to refresh partition metadata.

```
1 MSCK REPAIR TABLE flight_delays_pq;
```

Query the top 10 routes delayed by more than 1 hour.

```
1 SELECT origin, dest, count(*) as delays
2 FROM flight_delays_pq
3 WHERE depdelayminutes > 60
4 GROUP BY origin, dest
5 ORDER BY 3 DESC
6 LIMIT 10;
```

Note
The flight table data comes from Flights provided by US Department of Transportation, Bureau of Transportation Statistics. Desaturated from original.

Compression Formats

Athena supports the following compression formats:

- SNAPPY (Default compression format for files in the Parquet format)
- ZLIB. (Default compression format for files in the ORC format)
- GZIP
- LZO **Note**
  Use the GZIP compression in Athena for querying Amazon Kinesis Firehose logs. Athena and Amazon Kinesis Firehose each support different versions of SNAPPY, so GZIP is the only compatible format.

DDL and SQL Reference

Athena supports a subset of DDL statements and ANSI SQL functions and operators.

Topics

- Data Types
- DDL Statements
- SQL Queries, Functions, and Operators
- Unsupported DDL
- Limitations

Data Types

When you run **CREATE TABLE**, you must specify column names and their data types. For a complete syntax of this command, see CREATE TABLE.

The field `col_name` specifies the name for each column in the table Athena creates, along with the column's data type. If `col_name` begins with an underscore, enclose it in backticks, for example `_mycolumn`.

List of Supported Data Types in Athena

The `data_type` value in the `col_name` field of **CREATE TABLE** can be any of the following: +
primitive_type

- TINYINT

- SMALLINT

- INT. Athena combines two different implementations of the Integer data type. In Data Definition Language (DDL) queries, Athena uses the INT data type. In all other queries, Athena uses the INTEGER data type. In the JDBC driver, INTEGER is returned, to ensure compatibility with the business analytics applications.

- BIGINT

- BOOLEAN

- DOUBLE

- FLOAT

- STRING

- TIMESTAMP

- DECIMAL [(precision, scale)]

- DATE (not supported for Parquet file_format)

- CHAR. Fixed length character data, with a specified length between 1 and 255, such as `char(10)`. For more information, see CHAR Hive Data Type.

- VARCHAR. Variable length character data, with a specified length between 1 and 65535, such as `varchar (10)`. For more information, see VARCHAR Hive Data Type.

-

array_type

- ARRAY < data_type >

-

map_type

- MAP < primitive_type, data_type >

-

struct_type

- STRUCT < col_name : data_type [COMMENT col_comment] [, ...] >

For information about supported data type mappings between types in Athena, the JDBC driver, and Java data types, see the *"Data Types"* section in the JDBC Driver Installation and Configuration Guide.

DDL Statements

Use the following DDL statements directly in Athena.

Athena query engine is based on Hive DDL.

Athena does not support all DDL statements. For information, see Unsupported DDL.

Topics

- ALTER DATABASE SET DBPROPERTIES
- ALTER TABLE ADD PARTITION
- ALTER TABLE DROP PARTITION
- ALTER TABLE RENAME PARTITION
- ALTER TABLE SET LOCATION
- ALTER TABLE SET TBLPROPERTIES
- CREATE DATABASE
- CREATE TABLE
- CREATE VIEW
- DESCRIBE TABLE
- DESCRIBE VIEW
- DROP DATABASE
- DROP TABLE
- DROP VIEW
- MSCK REPAIR TABLE
- SHOW COLUMNS
- SHOW CREATE TABLE
- SHOW CREATE VIEW
- SHOW DATABASES
- SHOW PARTITIONS
- SHOW TABLES
- SHOW TBLPROPERTIES
- SHOW VIEWS

ALTER DATABASE SET DBPROPERTIES

Creates one or more properties for a database. The use of `DATABASE` and `SCHEMA` are interchangeable; they mean the same thing.

Synopsis

```
1 ALTER (DATABASE|SCHEMA) database_name
2   SET DBPROPERTIES ('property_name'='property_value' [, ...] )
```

Parameters

SET DBPROPERTIES ('property_name'='property_value' [, ...]
Specifies a property or properties for the database named `property_name` and establishes the value for each of the properties respectively as `property_value`. If `property_name` already exists, the old value is overwritten with `property_value`.

Examples

```
1 ALTER DATABASE jd_datasets
2   SET DBPROPERTIES ('creator'='John Doe', 'department'='applied mathematics');
```

```
1 ALTER SCHEMA jd_datasets
2   SET DBPROPERTIES ('creator'='Jane Doe');
```

ALTER TABLE ADD PARTITION

Creates one or more partition columns for the table. Each partition consists of one or more distinct column name/value combinations. A separate data directory is created for each specified combination, which can improve query performance in some circumstances. Partitioned columns don't exist within the table data itself, so if you use a column name that has the same name as a column in the table itself, you get an error. For more information, see Partitioning Data.

Synopsis

```
1  ALTER TABLE table_name ADD [IF NOT EXISTS]
2    PARTITION
3    (partition_col1_name = partition_col1_value
4    [,partition_col2_name = partition_col2_value]
5    [,...])
6    [LOCATION 'location1']
7    [PARTITION
8    (partition_colA_name = partition_colA_value
9    [,partition_colB_name = partition_colB_value
10   [,...])]
11   [LOCATION 'location2']
12   [,...]
```

Parameters

[IF NOT EXISTS]
Causes the error to be suppressed if a partition with the same definition already exists.

PARTITION (partition_col_name = partition_col_value [,...])
Creates a partition with the column name/value combinations that you specify. Enclose `partition_col_value` in string characters only if the data type of the column is a string.

[LOCATION 'location']
Specifies the directory in which to store the partitions defined by the preceding statement.

Examples

```
1 ALTER TABLE orders ADD
2   PARTITION (dt = '2016-05-14', country = 'IN');
```

```
1 ALTER TABLE orders ADD
2   PARTITION (dt = '2016-05-14', country = 'IN')
3   PARTITION (dt = '2016-05-15', country = 'IN');
```

```
1 ALTER TABLE orders ADD
2   PARTITION (dt = '2016-05-14', country = 'IN') LOCATION 's3://mystorage/path/to/
      INDIA_14_May_2016'
3   PARTITION (dt = '2016-05-15', country = 'IN') LOCATION 's3://mystorage/path/to/
      INDIA_15_May_2016';
```

ALTER TABLE DROP PARTITION

Drops one or more specified partitions for the named table.

Synopsis

```
1 ALTER TABLE table_name DROP [IF EXISTS] PARTITION (partition_spec) [, PARTITION (partition_spec)
   ]
```

Parameters

[IF EXISTS]
Suppresses the error message if the partition specified does not exist.

PARTITION (partition_spec)
Each `partition_spec` specifies a column name/value combination in the form `partition_col_name = partition_col_value [,...]`.

Examples

```
1 ALTER TABLE orders DROP PARTITION (dt = '2014-05-14', country = 'IN');
```

```
1 ALTER TABLE orders DROP PARTITION (dt = '2014-05-14', country = 'IN'), PARTITION (dt =
   '2014-05-15', country = 'IN');
```

ALTER TABLE RENAME PARTITION

Renames a partition column, `partition_spec`, for the table named `table_name`, to `new_partition_spec`.

Synopsis

```
1 ALTER TABLE table_name PARTITION (partition_spec) RENAME TO PARTITION (new_partition_spec)
```

Parameters

PARTITION (partition_spec)
Each `partition_spec` specifies a column name/value combination in the form `partition_col_name = partition_col_value [,...]`.

Examples

```
1 ALTER TABLE orders PARTITION (dt = '2014-05-14', country = 'IN') RENAME TO PARTITION (dt =
    '2014-05-15', country = 'IN');
```

ALTER TABLE SET LOCATION

Changes the location for the table named `table_name`, and optionally a partition with `partition_spec`.

Synopsis

```
1 ALTER TABLE table_name [ PARTITION (partition_spec) ] SET LOCATION 'new location'
```

Parameters

PARTITION (partition_spec)
Specifies the partition with parameters `partition_spec` whose location you want to change. The `partition_spec` specifies a column name/value combination in the form `partition_col_name = partition_col_value`.

SET LOCATION 'new location'
Specifies the new location, which must be an Amazon S3 location.

Examples

```
1 ALTER TABLE customers PARTITION (zip='98040', state='WA') SET LOCATION 's3://mystorage/custdata
    ';
```

ALTER TABLE SET TBLPROPERTIES

Adds custom metadata properties to a table sets their assigned values.

Managed tables are not supported, so setting 'EXTERNAL'='FALSE' has no effect.

Synopsis

```
1 ALTER TABLE table_name SET TBLPROPERTIES ('property_name' = 'property_value' [ , ... ])
```

Parameters

SET TBLPROPERTIES ('property_name' = 'property_value' [, ...])
Specifies the metadata properties to add as `property_name` and the value for each as `property value`. If `property_name` already exists, its value is reset to `property_value`.

Examples

```
1 ALTER TABLE orders SET TBLPROPERTIES ('notes'="Please don't drop this table.");
```

CREATE DATABASE

Creates a database. The use of `DATABASE` and `SCHEMA` is interchangeable. They mean the same thing.

Synopsis

```
1 CREATE (DATABASE|SCHEMA) [IF NOT EXISTS] database_name
2    [COMMENT 'database_comment']
3    [LOCATION 'S3_loc']
4    [WITH DBPROPERTIES ('property_name' = 'property_value') [, ...]]
```

Parameters

[IF NOT EXISTS]
Causes the error to be suppressed if a database named `database_name` already exists.

[COMMENT database_comment]
Establishes the metadata value for the built-in metadata property named `comment` and the value you provide for `database_comment`.

[LOCATION S3_loc]
Specifies the location where database files and metastore will exist as `S3_loc`. The location must be an Amazon S3 location.

[WITH DBPROPERTIES ('property_name' = 'property_value') [, ...]]
Allows you to specify custom metadata properties for the database definition.

Examples

```
1 CREATE DATABASE clickstreams;
```

```
1 CREATE DATABASE IF NOT EXISTS clickstreams
2    COMMENT 'Site Foo clickstream data aggregates'
3    LOCATION 's3://myS3location/clickstreams'
4    WITH DBPROPERTIES ('creator'='Jane D.', 'Dept.'='Marketing analytics');
```

CREATE TABLE

Creates a table with the name and the parameters that you specify.

Synopsis

```
1 CREATE [EXTERNAL] TABLE [IF NOT EXISTS]
2 [db_name.]table_name [(col_name data_type [COMMENT col_comment] [, ...] )]
3 [COMMENT table_comment]
4 [PARTITIONED BY (col_name data_type [COMMENT col_comment], ...)]
5 [ROW FORMAT row_format]
6 [STORED AS file_format] [WITH SERDEPROPERTIES (...)] ]
7 [LOCATION 's3_loc']
8 [TBLPROPERTIES ( ['has_encrypted_data'='true | false',] ['classification'='
      aws_glue_classification',] property_name=property_value [, ...] ) ]
```

Parameters

[EXTERNAL]
Specifies that the table is based on an underlying data file that exists in Amazon S3, in the `LOCATION` that you specify. When you create an external table, the data referenced must comply with the default format or the format that you specify with the `ROW FORMAT`, `STORED AS`, and `WITH SERDEPROPERTIES` clauses.

[IF NOT EXISTS]
Causes the error message to be suppressed if a table named `table_name` already exists.

[db_name.]table_name
Specifies a name for the table to be created. The optional `db_name` parameter specifies the database where the table exists. If omitted, the current database is assumed. If the table name includes numbers, enclose `table_name` in quotation marks, for example `"table123"`. If `table_name` begins with an underscore, use backticks, for example, `_mytable`. Special characters (other than underscore) are not supported.
Athena table names are case-insensitive; however, if you work with Apache Spark, Spark requires lowercase table names.

[(col_name data_type [COMMENT col_comment] [, ...])]
Specifies the name for each column to be created, along with the column's data type. Column names do not allow special characters other than underscore (_). If `col_name` begins with an underscore, enclose the column name in backticks, for example `_mycolumn`. The `data_type` value can be any of the following:
+

primitive_type

- TINYINT
- SMALLINT
- INT
- BIGINT
- BOOLEAN
- DOUBLE
- FLOAT
- STRING
- TIMESTAMP

- DECIMAL [(precision, scale)]

- DATE (not supported for Parquet file_format)

- CHAR. Fixed length character data, with a specified length between 1 and 255, such as `char(10)`. For more information, see CHAR Hive Data Type.

- VARCHAR. Variable length character data, with a specified length between 1 and 65535, such as `varchar (10)`. For more information, see VARCHAR Hive Data Type.

-

array_type

- ARRAY < data_type >

-

map_type

- MAP < primitive_type, data_type >

-

struct_type

- STRUCT < col_name : data_type [COMMENT col_comment] [, ...] >

[COMMENT table_comment]
Creates the `comment` table property and populates it with the `table_comment` you specify.

[PARTITIONED BY (col_name data_type [COMMENT col_comment], ...)]
Creates a partitioned table with one or more partition columns that have the `col_name`, `data_type` and `col_comment` specified. A table can have one or more partitions, which consist of a distinct column name and value combination. A separate data directory is created for each specified combination, which can improve query performance in some circumstances. Partitioned columns don't exist within the table data itself. If you use a value for `col_name` that is the same as a table column, you get an error. For more information, see Partitioning Data.
After you create a table with partitions, run a subsequent query that consists of the MSCK REPAIR TABLE clause to refresh partition metadata, for example, `MSCK REPAIR TABLE cloudfront_logs;`.

[ROW FORMAT row_format]
Specifies the row format of the table and its underlying source data if applicable. For `row_format`, you can specify one or more delimiters with the `DELIMITED` clause or, alternatively, use the `SERDE` clause as described below. If `ROW FORMAT` is omitted or `ROW FORMAT DELIMITED` is specified, a native SerDe is used.

- [DELIMITED FIELDS TERMINATED BY char [ESCAPED BY char]]

- [DELIMITED COLLECTION ITEMS TERMINATED BY char]

- [MAP KEYS TERMINATED BY char]

- [LINES TERMINATED BY char]

- [NULL DEFINED AS char] -- (Note: Available in Hive 0.13 and later) **--OR--**

- SERDE 'serde_name' [WITH SERDEPROPERTIES ("property_name" = "property_value", "property_name" = "property_value" [, ...])]

   The `serde_name` indicates the SerDe to use. The `WITH SERDEPROPERTIES` clause allows you to provide one or more custom properties allowed by the SerDe.

[STORED AS file_format]
Specifies the file format for table data. If omitted, `TEXTFILE` is the default. Options for `file_format` are:

- SEQUENCEFILE

- TEXTFILE
- RCFILE
- ORC
- PARQUET
- AVRO
- INPUTFORMAT input_format_classname OUTPUTFORMAT output_format_classname

[LOCATION 'S3_loc']

Specifies the location of the underlying data in Amazon S3 from which the table is created, for example, `s3://mystorage/`. For more information about considerations such as data format and permissions, see Requirements for Tables in Athena and Data in Amazon S3.

Use a trailing slash for your folder or bucket. Do not use file names or glob characters.

Use: `s3://mybucket/myfolder/`

Don't use: `s3://path_to_bucket s3://path_to_bucket/* s3://path_to-bucket/mydatafile.dat`

[TBLPROPERTIES (['has_encrypted_data'='true | false',] ['classification'='aws_glue_classification',] property_name=property_value [, ...])]

Specifies custom metadata key-value pairs for the table definition in addition to predefined table properties, such as `"comment"`.

Athena has a built-in property, `has_encrypted_data`. Set this property to `true` to indicate that the underlying dataset specified by `LOCATION` is encrypted. If omitted, `false` is assumed. If omitted or set to `false` when underlying data is encrypted, the query results in an error. For more information, see Configuring Encryption Options.

To run ETL jobs, AWS Glue requires that you create a table with the `classification` property to indicate the data type for AWS Glue as `csv`, `parquet`, `orc`, `avro`, or `json`. For example, `'classification'='csv'`. ETL jobs will fail if you do not specify this property. You can subsequently specify it using the AWS Glue console, API, or CLI. For more information, see Using AWS Glue Jobs for ETL with Athena and Authoring Jobs in Glue in the *AWS Glue Developer Guide*.

Examples

```
1  CREATE EXTERNAL TABLE IF NOT EXISTS mydatabase.cloudfront_logs (
2    Date DATE,
3    Time STRING,
4    Location STRING,
5    Bytes INT,
6    RequestIP STRING,
7    Method STRING,
8    Host STRING,
9    Uri STRING,
10   Status INT,
11   Referrer STRING,
12   os STRING,
13   Browser STRING,
14   BrowserVersion STRING
15       ) ROW FORMAT SERDE 'org.apache.hadoop.hive.serde2.RegexSerDe'
16       WITH SERDEPROPERTIES (
17       "input.regex" = "^(?!#)([^ ]+)\\s+([^ ]+)\\s+([^ ]+)\\s+([^ ]+)\\s+([^ ]+)\\s+([^ ]+)\\s
             +([^ ]+)\\s+([^ ]+)\\s+([^ ]+)\\s+([^ ]+)\\s+[^\(]+[\(]([^\;]+).*\%20([^\/]+)[\/](.*)$
             "
18       ) LOCATION 's3://athena-examples/cloudfront/plaintext/';
```

CREATE VIEW

Creates a new view from a specified **SELECT** query. The view is a logical table that can be referenced by future queries. Views do not contain any data and do not write data. Instead, the query specified by the view runs each time you reference the view by another query.

The optional **OR REPLACE** clause lets you update the existing view by replacing it. For more information, see Creating Views.

Synopsis

```
1 CREATE [ OR REPLACE ] VIEW view_name AS query
```

Examples

To create a view **test** from the table **orders**, use a query similar to the following:

```
1 CREATE VIEW test AS
2 SELECT
3 orderkey,
4 orderstatus,
5 totalprice / 2 AS half
6 FROM orders
```

To create a view **orders_by_date** from the table **orders**, use the following query:

```
1 CREATE VIEW orders_by_date AS
2 SELECT orderdate, sum(totalprice) AS price
3 FROM orders
4 GROUP BY orderdate
```

To update an existing view, use an example similar to the following:

```
1 CREATE OR REPLACE VIEW test AS
2 SELECT orderkey, orderstatus, totalprice / 4 AS quarter
3 FROM orders
```

See also SHOW COLUMNS, SHOW CREATE VIEW, DESCRIBE VIEW, and DROP VIEW.

DESCRIBE TABLE

Shows the list of columns, including partition columns, for the named column. This allows you to examine the attributes of a complex column.

Synopsis

```
1 DESCRIBE [EXTENDED | FORMATTED] [db_name.]table_name [PARTITION partition_spec] [col_name ( [.
    field_name] | [.'$elem$'] | [.'$key$'] | [.'$value$'] )]
```

Parameters

[EXTENDED | FORMATTED]
Determines the format of the output. If you specify EXTENDED, all metadata for the table is output in Thrift serialized form. This is useful primarily for debugging and not for general use. Use FORMATTED or omit the clause to show the metadata in tabular format.

[PARTITION partition_spec]
Lists the metadata for the partition with partition_spec if included.

[col_name ([.field_name] | [.'$elem$'] | [.'key'] | [.'$value$'])*]
Specifies the column and attributes to examine. You can specify .field_name for an element of a struct, '$elem$' for array element, 'key' for a map key, and '$value$' for map value. You can specify this recursively to further explore the complex column.

Examples

```
1 DESCRIBE orders;
```

DESCRIBE VIEW

Shows the list of columns for the named view. This allows you to examine the attributes of a complex view.

Synopsis

```
1 DESCRIBE [view_name]
```

Example

```
1 DESCRIBE orders;
```

See also SHOW COLUMNS, SHOW CREATE VIEW, SHOW VIEWS, and DROP VIEW.

DROP DATABASE

Removes the named database from the catalog. If the database contains tables, you must either drop the tables before executing DROP DATABASE or use the CASCADE clause. The use of DATABASE and SCHEMA are interchangeable. They mean the same thing.

Synopsis

```
1 DROP {DATABASE | SCHEMA} [IF EXISTS] database_name [RESTRICT | CASCADE]
```

Parameters

[IF EXISTS]
Causes the error to be suppressed if `database_name` doesn't exist.

[RESTRICT|CASCADE]
Determines how tables within `database_name` are regarded during the DROP operation. If you specify RESTRICT, the database is not dropped if it contains tables. This is the default behavior. Specifying CASCADE causes the database and all its tables to be dropped.

Examples

```
1 DROP DATABASE clickstreams;
```

```
1 DROP SCHEMA IF EXISTS clickstreams CASCADE;
```

DROP TABLE

Removes the metadata table definition for the table named `table_name`. When you drop an external table, the underlying data remains intact because all tables in Athena are EXTERNAL.

Synopsis

```
1 DROP TABLE [IF EXISTS] table_name [PURGE]
```

Parameters

[IF EXISTS]
Causes the error to be suppressed if `table_name` doesn't exist.

[PURGE]
Applies to managed tables. Ignored for external tables. Specifies that data should be removed permanently rather than being moved to the `.Trash/Current` directory.

Examples

```
1 DROP TABLE fulfilled_orders;
```

```
1 DROP TABLE IF EXISTS fulfilled_orders PURGE;
```

DROP VIEW

Drops (deletes) an existing view. The optional IF EXISTS clause causes the error to be suppressed if the view does not exist.

For more information, see Deleting Views.

Synopsis

```
1 DROP VIEW [ IF EXISTS ] view_name
```

Examples

```
1 DROP VIEW orders_by_date
```

```
1 DROP VIEW IF EXISTS orders_by_date
```

See also CREATE VIEW, SHOW COLUMNS, SHOW CREATE VIEW, SHOW VIEWS, and DESCRIBE VIEW.

MSCK REPAIR TABLE

Recovers partitions and data associated with partitions. Use this statement when you add partitions to the catalog. It is possible it will take some time to add all partitions. If this operation times out, it will be in an incomplete state where only a few partitions are added to the catalog. You should run the statement on the same table until all partitions are added. For more information, see Partitioning Data.

Synopsis

```
1 MSCK REPAIR TABLE table_name
```

Examples

```
1 MSCK REPAIR TABLE orders;
```

SHOW COLUMNS

Lists the columns in the schema for a base table or a view.

Synopsis

```
1 SHOW COLUMNS IN table_name|view_name
```

Examples

```
1 SHOW COLUMNS IN clicks;
```

SHOW CREATE TABLE

Analyzes an existing table named table_name to generate the query that created it.

Synopsis

```
1 SHOW CREATE TABLE [db_name.]table_name
```

Parameters

TABLE [db_name.]table_name
The db_name parameter is optional. If omitted, the context defaults to the current database.

Examples

```
1 SHOW CREATE TABLE orderclickstoday;
```

```
1 SHOW CREATE TABLE salesdata.orderclickstoday;
```

SHOW CREATE VIEW

Shows the SQL statement that creates the specified view.

Synopsis

```
1 SHOW CREATE VIEW view_name
```

Examples

```
1 SHOW CREATE VIEW orders_by_date
```

See also CREATE VIEW and DROP VIEW.

SHOW DATABASES

Lists all databases defined in the metastore. You can use DATABASES or SCHEMAS. They mean the same thing.

Synopsis

```
1 SHOW {DATABASES | SCHEMAS} [LIKE 'regular_expression']
```

Parameters

[LIKE 'regular_expression']
Filters the list of databases to those that match the regular_expression you specify. Wildcards can only be *, which indicates any character, or |, which indicates a choice between characters.

Examples

```
1 SHOW SCHEMAS;
```

```
1 SHOW DATABASES LIKE '*analytics';
```

SHOW PARTITIONS

Lists all the partitions in a table.

Synopsis

```
1 SHOW PARTITIONS table_name
```

Examples

```
1 SHOW PARTITIONS clicks;
```

SHOW TABLES

Lists all the base tables and views in a database.

Synopsis

```
1 SHOW TABLES [IN database_name] ['regular_expression']
```

Parameters

[IN database_name]
Specifies the `database_name` from which tables will be listed. If omitted, the database from the current context is assumed.

['regular_expression']
Filters the list of tables to those that match the `regular_expression` you specify. Only the wildcard *, which indicates any character, or |, which indicates a choice between characters, can be used.

Examples

```
1 SHOW TABLES;
```

```
1 SHOW TABLES IN marketing_analytics 'orders*';
```

SHOW TBLPROPERTIES

Lists table properties for the named table.

Synopsis

```
1 SHOW TBLPROPERTIES table_name [('property_name')]
```

Parameters

[('property_name')]
If included, only the value of the property named `property_name` is listed.

Examples

```
1 SHOW TBLPROPERTIES orders;
```

```
1 SHOW TBLPROPERTIES orders('comment');
```

SHOW VIEWS

Lists the views in the specified database, or in the current database if you omit the database name. Use the optional `LIKE` clause with a regular expression to restrict the list of view names.

Athena returns a list of `STRING` type values where each value is a view name.

Synopsis

```
1 SHOW VIEWS [IN database_name] LIKE ['regular_expression']
```

Parameters

[IN database_name]
Specifies the `database_name` from which views will be listed. If omitted, the database from the current context is assumed.

[LIKE 'regular_expression']
Filters the list of views to those that match the `regular_expression` you specify. Only the wildcard *, which indicates any character, or |, which indicates a choice between characters, can be used.

Examples

```
1 SHOW VIEWS;
```

```
1 SHOW VIEWS IN marketing_analytics LIKE 'orders*';
```

See also SHOW COLUMNS, SHOW CREATE VIEW, DESCRIBE VIEW, and DROP VIEW.

SQL Queries, Functions, and Operators

Use the following functions directly in Athena.

Amazon Athena query engine is based on Presto 0.172. For more information about these functions, see Presto 0.172 Functions and Operators.

Athena does not support all of Presto's features. For information, see Limitations.

219

- SELECT
- Logical Operators
- Comparison Functions and Operators
- Conditional Expressions
- Conversion Functions
- Mathematical Functions and Operators
- Bitwise Functions
- Decimal Functions and Operators
- String Functions and Operators
- Binary Functions
- Date and Time Functions and Operators
- Regular Expression Functions
- JSON Functions and Operators
- URL Functions
- Aggregate Functions
- Window Functions
- Color Functions
- Array Functions and Operators
- Map Functions and Operators
- Lambda Expressions and Functions
- Teradata Functions

SELECT

Retrieves rows from zero or more tables.

Synopsis

```
1  [ WITH with_query [, ...] ]
2  SELECT [ ALL | DISTINCT ] select_expression [, ...]
3  [ FROM from_item [, ...] ]
4  [ WHERE condition ]
5  [ GROUP BY [ ALL | DISTINCT ] grouping_element [, ...] ]
6  [ HAVING condition ]
7  [ UNION [ ALL | DISTINCT ] union_query ]
8  [ ORDER BY expression [ ASC | DESC ] [ NULLS FIRST | NULLS LAST] [, ...] ]
9  [ LIMIT [ count | ALL ] ]
```

Parameters

[WITH with_query [, ...]]

You can use WITH to flatten nested queries, or to simplify subqueries.

Using the WITH clause to create recursive queries is not supported.

The WITH clause precedes the SELECT list in a query and defines one or more subqueries for use within the SELECT query.

Each subquery defines a temporary table, similar to a view definition, which you can reference in the FROM clause. The tables are used only when the query runs.

with_query syntax is:

```
1  subquery_table_name [ ( column_name [, ...] ) ] AS (subquery)
```

Where:

- subquery_table_name is a unique name for a temporary table that defines the results of the WITH clause subquery. Each subquery must have a table name that can be referenced in the FROM clause.
- column_name [, ...] is an optional list of output column names. The number of column names must be equal to or less than the number of columns defined by subquery.
- subquery is any query statement.

[ALL | DISTINCT] select_expr

select_expr determines the rows to be selected.

ALL is the default. Using ALL is treated the same as if it were omitted; all rows for all columns are selected and duplicates are kept.

Use DISTINCT to return only distinct values when a column contains duplicate values.

FROM from_item [, ...]

Indicates the input to the query, where from_item can be a view, a join construct, or a subquery as described below.

The from_item can be either:

- table_name [[AS] alias [(column_alias [, ...])]]

Where table_name is the name of the target table from which to select rows, alias is the name to give the output of the SELECT statement, and column_alias defines the columns for the alias specified. **-OR-**

- join_type from_item [ON join_condition | USING (join_column [, ...])]

Where join_type is one of:

- [INNER] JOIN
- LEFT [OUTER] JOIN
- RIGHT [OUTER] JOIN
- FULL [OUTER] JOIN
- CROSS JOIN
- ON join_condition | USING (join_column [, ...]) Where using join_condition allows you to specify column names for join keys in multiple tables, and using join_column requires join_column to exist in both tables.

[WHERE condition]

Filters results according to the condition you specify.

[GROUP BY [ALL | DISTINCT] grouping_expressions [, ...]]

Divides the output of the SELECT statement into rows with matching values.

ALL and DISTINCT determine whether duplicate grouping sets each produce distinct output rows. If omitted, ALL is assumed.

grouping_expressions allow you to perform complex grouping operations.

The grouping_expressions element can be any function, such as SUM, AVG, or COUNT, performed on input columns, or be an ordinal number that selects an output column by position, starting at one.

GROUP BY expressions can group output by input column names that don't appear in the output of the SELECT statement.

All output expressions must be either aggregate functions or columns present in the GROUP BY clause.

You can use a single query to perform analysis that requires aggregating multiple column sets.

These complex grouping operations don't support expressions comprising input columns. Only column names or ordinals are allowed.

You can often use UNION ALL to achieve the same results as these GROUP BY operations, but queries that use GROUP BY have the advantage of reading the data one time, whereas UNION ALL reads the underlying data three times and may produce inconsistent results when the data source is subject to change.

GROUP BY CUBE generates all possible grouping sets for a given set of columns. GROUP BY ROLLUP generates all possible subtotals for a given set of columns.

[HAVING condition]

Used with aggregate functions and the GROUP BY clause. Controls which groups are selected, eliminating groups that don't satisfy condition. This filtering occurs after groups and aggregates are computed.

[UNION [ALL | DISTINCT] union_query]]

Combines the results of more than one SELECT statement into a single query. ALL or DISTINCT control which rows are included in the final result set.

ALL causes all rows to be included, even if the rows are identical.

DISTINCT causes only unique rows to be included in the combined result set. DISTINCT is the default.

Multiple UNION clauses are processed left to right unless you use parentheses to explicitly define the order of processing.

[ORDER BY expression [ASC | DESC] [NULLS FIRST | NULLS LAST] [, ...]]

Sorts a result set by one or more output expression.

When the clause contains multiple expressions, the result set is sorted according to the first expression. Then the second expression is applied to rows that have matching values from the first expression, and so on.

Each expression may specify output columns from SELECT or an ordinal number for an output column by position, starting at one.

ORDER BY is evaluated as the last step after any GROUP BY or HAVING clause. ASC and DESC determine whether results are sorted in ascending or descending order.

The default null ordering is NULLS LAST, regardless of ascending or descending sort order.

LIMIT [count | ALL]

Restricts the number of rows in the result set to count. LIMIT ALL is the same as omitting the LIMIT clause. If the query has no ORDER BY clause, the results are arbitrary.

TABLESAMPLE BERNOULLI | SYSTEM (percentage)

Optional operator to select rows from a table based on a sampling method.
`BERNOULLI` selects each row to be in the table sample with a probability of `percentage`. All physical blocks of the table are scanned, and certain rows are skipped based on a comparison between the sample `percentage` and a random value calculated at runtime.

With `SYSTEM`, the table is divided into logical segments of data, and the table is sampled at this granularity. Either all rows from a particular segment are selected, or the segment is skipped based on a comparison between the sample `percentage` and a random value calculated at runtime. `SYTSTEM` sampling is dependent on the connector. This method does not guarantee independent sampling probabilities.

[UNNEST (array_or_map) [WITH ORDINALITY]]
Expands an array or map into a relation. Arrays are expanded into a single column. Maps are expanded into two columns (*key*, *value*).

You can use `UNNEST` with multiple arguments, which are expanded into multiple columns with as many rows as the highest cardinality argument.

Other columns are padded with nulls.

The `WITH ORDINALITY` clause adds an ordinality column to the end.

`UNNEST` is usually used with a `JOIN` and can reference columns from relations on the left side of the `JOIN`.

Examples

```
1 SELECT * FROM table;
```

```
1 SELECT os, COUNT(*) count FROM cloudfront_logs WHERE date BETWEEN date '2014-07-05' AND date
    '2014-08-05' GROUP BY os;
```

For more examples, see Querying Data in Amazon Athena Tables.

Unsupported DDL

The following native Hive DDLs are not supported by Athena:

- ALTER INDEX
- ALTER TABLE table_name ARCHIVE PARTITION
- ALTER TABLE table_name CLUSTERED BY
- ALTER TABLE table_name EXCHANGE PARTITION
- ALTER TABLE table_name NOT CLUSTERED
- ALTER TABLE table_name NOT SKEWED
- ALTER TABLE table_name NOT SORTED
- ALTER TABLE table_name NOT STORED AS DIRECTORIES
- ALTER TABLE table_name partitionSpec ADD COLUMNS
- ALTER TABLE table_name partitionSpec CHANGE COLUMNS
- ALTER TABLE table_name partitionSpec COMPACT
- ALTER TABLE table_name partitionSpec CONCATENATE
- ALTER TABLE table_name partitionSpec REPLACE COLUMNS
- ALTER TABLE table_name partitionSpec SET FILEFORMAT
- ALTER TABLE table_name RENAME TO
- ALTER TABLE table_name SET SKEWED LOCATION
- ALTER TABLE table_name SKEWED BY
- ALTER TABLE table_name TOUCH
- ALTER TABLE table_name UNARCHIVE PARTITION
- COMMIT
- CREATE INDEX
- CREATE ROLE
- CREATE TABLE table_name LIKE existing_table_name

- CREATE TEMPORARY MACRO
- DELETE FROM
- DESCRIBE DATABASE
- DFS
- DROP INDEX
- DROP ROLE
- DROP TEMPORARY MACRO
- EXPORT TABLE
- GRANT ROLE
- IMPORT TABLE
- INSERT INTO
- LOCK DATABASE
- LOCK TABLE
- REVOKE ROLE
- ROLLBACK
- SHOW COMPACTIONS
- SHOW CURRENT ROLES
- SHOW GRANT
- SHOW INDEXES
- SHOW LOCKS
- SHOW PRINCIPALS
- SHOW ROLE GRANT
- SHOW ROLES
- SHOW TRANSACTIONS
- START TRANSACTION
- UNLOCK DATABASE
- UNLOCK TABLE

Limitations

Athena does not support the following features, which are supported by an open source Presto version 0.172.

- User-defined functions (UDFs or UDAFs).
- Stored procedures.
- A particular subset of data types is supported. For more information, see Data Types.
- `CREATE TABLE AS SELECT` statements.
- `INSERT INTO` statements.
- Prepared statements. You cannot run `EXECUTE` with `USING`.
- `CREATE TABLE LIKE`.
- `DESCRIBE INPUT` and `DESCRIBE OUTPUT`.
- `EXPLAIN` statements.
- Federated connectors. For more information, see Connectors.

Code Samples, Service Limits, and Previous JDBC Driver

Use the following examples to create Athena applications based on AWS SDK for Java.

Use the links in this section to use the previous version of the JDBC driver.

Learn about service limits.

Topics

- Code Samples
- Using the Previous Version of the JDBC Driver
- Service Limits

Code Samples

Use examples in this topic as a starting point for writing Athena applications using the AWS SDK for Java. +
Java Code Samples

- Create a Client to Access Athena

-

Working with Query Executions
+ Start Query Execution + Stop Query Execution + List Query Executions +
Working with Named Queries
+ Create a Named Query + Delete a Named Query + List Query Executions

Note
These samples use constants (for example, `ATHENA_SAMPLE_QUERY`) for strings, which are defined in an
`ExampleConstants` class declaration not shown in this topic. Replace these constants with your own strings or
defined constants.

Create a Client to Access Athena

```
1 package com.amazonaws.services.athena.sdksamples;
2
3 import com.amazonaws.ClientConfiguration;
4 import com.amazonaws.auth.InstanceProfileCredentialsProvider;
5 import com.amazonaws.regions.Regions;
6 import com.amazonaws.services.athena.AmazonAthena;
7 import com.amazonaws.services.athena.AmazonAthenaClientBuilder;
8
9 /**
10 * AthenaClientFactory
11 * ------------------------------------
12 * This code shows how to create and configure an Amazon Athena client.
13 */
14 public class AthenaClientFactory
15 {
16   /**
17    * AmazonAthenaClientBuilder to build Athena with the following properties:
18    * - Set the region of the client
19    * - Use the instance profile from the EC2 instance as the credentials provider
20    * - Configure the client to increase the execution timeout.
21    */
22   private final AmazonAthenaClientBuilder builder = AmazonAthenaClientBuilder.standard()
23           .withRegion(Regions.US_EAST_1)
24           .withCredentials(InstanceProfileCredentialsProvider.getInstance())
25           .withClientConfiguration(new ClientConfiguration().withClientExecutionTimeout(
26               ExampleConstants.CLIENT_EXECUTION_TIMEOUT));
27   public AmazonAthena createClient()
28   {
29       return builder.build();
30   }
31 }
```

Start Query Execution

```java
1 package com.amazonaws.services.athena.sdksamples;
2
3 import com.amazonaws.services.athena.AmazonAthena;
4 import com.amazonaws.services.athena.model.ColumnInfo;
5 import com.amazonaws.services.athena.model.GetQueryExecutionRequest;
6 import com.amazonaws.services.athena.model.GetQueryExecutionResult;
7 import com.amazonaws.services.athena.model.GetQueryResultsRequest;
8 import com.amazonaws.services.athena.model.GetQueryResultsResult;
9 import com.amazonaws.services.athena.model.QueryExecutionContext;
10 import com.amazonaws.services.athena.model.QueryExecutionState;
11 import com.amazonaws.services.athena.model.ResultConfiguration;
12 import com.amazonaws.services.athena.model.Row;
13 import com.amazonaws.services.athena.model.StartQueryExecutionRequest;
14 import com.amazonaws.services.athena.model.StartQueryExecutionResult;
15
16 import java.util.List;
17
18 /**
19 * StartQueryExample
20 * -------------------------------------
21 * This code shows how to submit a query to Athena for execution, wait till results
22 * are available, and then process the results.
23 */
24 public class StartQueryExample
25 {
26   public static void main(String[] args) throws InterruptedException
27   {
28       // Build an AmazonAthena client
29       AthenaClientFactory factory = new AthenaClientFactory();
30       AmazonAthena client = factory.createClient();
31
32       String queryExecutionId = submitAthenaQuery(client);
33
34       waitForQueryToComplete(client, queryExecutionId);
35
36       processResultRows(client, queryExecutionId);
37   }
38
39   /**
40    * Submits a sample query to Athena and returns the execution ID of the query.
41    */
42   private static String submitAthenaQuery(AmazonAthena client)
43   {
44       // The QueryExecutionContext allows us to set the Database.
45       QueryExecutionContext queryExecutionContext = new QueryExecutionContext().withDatabase(
46           ExampleConstants.ATHENA_DEFAULT_DATABASE);
47
48       // The result configuration specifies where the results of the query should go in S3 and
49           encryption options
50       ResultConfiguration resultConfiguration = new ResultConfiguration()
51               // You can provide encryption options for the output that is written.
52               // .withEncryptionConfiguration(encryptionConfiguration)
```

```
51          .withOutputLocation(ExampleConstants.ATHENA_OUTPUT_BUCKET);
52
53      // Create the StartQueryExecutionRequest to send to Athena which will start the query.
54      StartQueryExecutionRequest startQueryExecutionRequest = new StartQueryExecutionRequest()
55              .withQueryString(ExampleConstants.ATHENA_SAMPLE_QUERY)
56              .withQueryExecutionContext(queryExecutionContext)
57              .withResultConfiguration(resultConfiguration);
58
59      StartQueryExecutionResult startQueryExecutionResult = client.startQueryExecution(
            startQueryExecutionRequest);
60      return startQueryExecutionResult.getQueryExecutionId();
61  }
62
63  /**
64   * Wait for an Athena query to complete, fail or to be cancelled. This is done by polling
        Athena over an
65   * interval of time. If a query fails or is cancelled, then it will throw an exception.
66   */
67
68      private static void waitForQueryToComplete(AmazonAthena client, String queryExecutionId)
                throws InterruptedException
69  {
70      GetQueryExecutionRequest getQueryExecutionRequest = new GetQueryExecutionRequest()
71              .withQueryExecutionId(queryExecutionId);
72
73      GetQueryExecutionResult getQueryExecutionResult = null;
74      boolean isQueryStillRunning = true;
75      while (isQueryStillRunning) {
76          getQueryExecutionResult = client.getQueryExecution(getQueryExecutionRequest);
77          String queryState = getQueryExecutionResult.getQueryExecution().getStatus().getState()
                ;
78          if (queryState.equals(QueryExecutionState.FAILED.toString())) {
79              throw new RuntimeException("Query Failed to run with Error Message: " +
                    getQueryExecutionResult.getQueryExecution().getStatus().getStateChangeReason()
                    );
80          }
81          else if (queryState.equals(QueryExecutionState.CANCELLED.toString())) {
82              throw new RuntimeException("Query was cancelled.");
83          }
84          else if (queryState.equals(QueryExecutionState.SUCCEEDED.toString())) {
85              isQueryStillRunning = false;
86          }
87          else {
88              // Sleep an amount of time before retrying again.
89              Thread.sleep(ExampleConstants.SLEEP_AMOUNT_IN_MS);
90          }
91          System.out.println("Current Status is: " + queryState);
92      }
93  }
94
95  /**
96   * This code calls Athena and retrieves the results of a query.
97   * The query must be in a completed state before the results can be retrieved and
98   * paginated. The first row of results are the column headers.
```

```java
 99    */
100   private static void processResultRows(AmazonAthena client, String queryExecutionId)
101   {
102       GetQueryResultsRequest getQueryResultsRequest = new GetQueryResultsRequest()
103               // Max Results can be set but if its not set,
104               // it will choose the maximum page size
105               // As of the writing of this code, the maximum value is 1000
106               // .withMaxResults(1000)
107               .withQueryExecutionId(queryExecutionId);
108
109       GetQueryResultsResult getQueryResultsResult = client.getQueryResults(
110           getQueryResultsRequest);
110       List<ColumnInfo> columnInfoList = getQueryResultsResult.getResultSet().
               getResultSetMetadata().getColumnInfo();
111
112       while (true) {
113           List<Row> results = getQueryResultsResult.getResultSet().getRows();
114           for (Row row : results) {
115               // Process the row. The first row of the first page holds the column names.
116               processRow(row, columnInfoList);
117           }
118           // If nextToken is null, there are no more pages to read. Break out of the loop.
119           if (getQueryResultsResult.getNextToken() == null) {
120               break;
121           }
122           getQueryResultsResult = client.getQueryResults(
123                   getQueryResultsRequest.withNextToken(getQueryResultsResult.getNextToken()));
124       }
125   }
126
127   private static void processRow(Row row, List<ColumnInfo> columnInfoList)
128   {
129       for (int i = 0; i < columnInfoList.size(); ++i) {
130           switch (columnInfoList.get(i).getType()) {
131               case "varchar":
132                   // Convert and Process as String
133                   break;
134               case "tinyint":
135                   // Convert and Process as tinyint
136                   break;
137               case "smallint":
138                   // Convert and Process as smallint
139                   break;
140               case "integer":
141                   // Convert and Process as integer
142                   break;
143               case "bigint":
144                   // Convert and Process as bigint
145                   break;
146               case "double":
147                   // Convert and Process as double
148                   break;
149               case "boolean":
150                   // Convert and Process as boolean
```

```
151            break;
152          case "date":
153            // Convert and Process as date
154            break;
155          case "timestamp":
156            // Convert and Process as timestamp
157            break;
158          default:
159            throw new RuntimeException("Unexpected Type is not expected" + columnInfoList.
                 get(i).getType());
160        }
161      }
162    }
163 }
```

Stop Query Execution

```
 1 package com.amazonaws.services.athena.sdksamples;
 2
 3 import com.amazonaws.services.athena.AmazonAthena;
 4 import com.amazonaws.services.athena.model.GetQueryExecutionRequest;
 5 import com.amazonaws.services.athena.model.GetQueryExecutionResult;
 6 import com.amazonaws.services.athena.model.QueryExecutionContext;
 7 import com.amazonaws.services.athena.model.ResultConfiguration;
 8 import com.amazonaws.services.athena.model.StartQueryExecutionRequest;
 9 import com.amazonaws.services.athena.model.StartQueryExecutionResult;
10 import com.amazonaws.services.athena.model.StopQueryExecutionRequest;
11 import com.amazonaws.services.athena.model.StopQueryExecutionResult;
12
13 /**
14 * StopQueryExecutionExample
15 * --------------------------------------
16 * This code runs an example query, immediately stops the query, and checks the status of the
      query to
17 * ensure that it was cancelled.
18 */
19 public class StopQueryExecutionExample
20 {
21   public static void main(String[] args) throws Exception
22   {
23       // Build an Athena client
24       AthenaClientFactory factory = new AthenaClientFactory();
25       AmazonAthena client = factory.createClient();
26
27       String sampleQueryExecutionId = getExecutionId(client);
28
29       // Submit the stop query Request
30       StopQueryExecutionRequest stopQueryExecutionRequest = new StopQueryExecutionRequest()
31             .withQueryExecutionId(sampleQueryExecutionId);
32
33       StopQueryExecutionResult stopQueryExecutionResult = client.stopQueryExecution(
            stopQueryExecutionRequest);
34
35       // Ensure that the query was stopped
```

```
36    GetQueryExecutionRequest getQueryExecutionRequest = new GetQueryExecutionRequest()
37            .withQueryExecutionId(sampleQueryExecutionId);
38
39    GetQueryExecutionResult getQueryExecutionResult = client.getQueryExecution(
          getQueryExecutionRequest);
40    if (getQueryExecutionResult.getQueryExecution().getStatus().getState().equals(
          ExampleConstants.QUERY_STATE_CANCELLED)) {
41        // Query was cancelled.
42        System.out.println("Query has been cancelled");
43    }
44  }
45
46  /**
47   * Submits an example query and returns a query execution ID of a running query to stop.
48   */
49  public static String getExecutionId(AmazonAthena client)
50  {
51    QueryExecutionContext queryExecutionContext = new QueryExecutionContext().withDatabase(
          ExampleConstants.ATHENA_DEFAULT_DATABASE);
52
53    ResultConfiguration resultConfiguration = new ResultConfiguration()
54            .withOutputLocation(ExampleConstants.ATHENA_OUTPUT_BUCKET);
55
56    StartQueryExecutionRequest startQueryExecutionRequest = new StartQueryExecutionRequest()
57            .withQueryString(ExampleConstants.ATHENA_SAMPLE_QUERY)
58            .withQueryExecutionContext(queryExecutionContext)
59            .withResultConfiguration(resultConfiguration);
60
61    StartQueryExecutionResult startQueryExecutionResult = client.startQueryExecution(
          startQueryExecutionRequest);
62
63    return startQueryExecutionResult.getQueryExecutionId();
64  }
65 }
```

List Query Executions

```
1 package com.amazonaws.services.athena.sdksamples;
2
3 import com.amazonaws.services.athena.AmazonAthena;
4 import com.amazonaws.services.athena.model.ListQueryExecutionsRequest;
5 import com.amazonaws.services.athena.model.ListQueryExecutionsResult;
6
7 import java.util.List;
8
9 /**
10 * ListQueryExecutionsExample
11 * -------------------------------------
12 * This code shows how to obtain a list of query execution IDs.
13 */
14 public class ListQueryExecutionsExample
15 {
16   public static void main(String[] args) throws Exception
17   {
```

```
18      // Build an Athena client
19      AthenaClientFactory factory = new AthenaClientFactory();
20      AmazonAthena client = factory.createClient();
21
22      // Build the request
23      ListQueryExecutionsRequest listQueryExecutionsRequest = new ListQueryExecutionsRequest();
24
25      // Get the list results.
26      ListQueryExecutionsResult listQueryExecutionsResult = client.listQueryExecutions(
            listQueryExecutionsRequest);
27
28      // Process the results.
29      boolean hasMoreResults = true;
30      while (hasMoreResults) {
31          List<String> queryExecutionIds = listQueryExecutionsResult.getQueryExecutionIds();
32          // process queryExecutionIds.
33
34          //If nextToken is not null, then there are more results. Get the next page of results.
35          if (listQueryExecutionsResult.getNextToken() != null) {
36              listQueryExecutionsResult = client.listQueryExecutions(
37                      listQueryExecutionsRequest.withNextToken(listQueryExecutionsResult.
                            getNextToken()));
38          }
39          else {
40              hasMoreResults = false;
41          }
42      }
43    }
44 }
```

Create a Named Query

```
1 package com.amazonaws.services.athena.sdksamples;
2
3 import com.amazonaws.services.athena.AmazonAthena;
4 import com.amazonaws.services.athena.model.CreateNamedQueryRequest;
5 import com.amazonaws.services.athena.model.CreateNamedQueryResult;
6
7 /**
8 * CreateNamedQueryExample
9 * ------------------------------------
10 * This code shows how to create a named query.
11 */
12 public class CreateNamedQueryExample
13 {
14   public static void main(String[] args) throws Exception
15   {
16       // Build an Athena client
17       AthenaClientFactory factory = new AthenaClientFactory();
18       AmazonAthena client = factory.createClient();
19
20       // Create the named query request.
21       CreateNamedQueryRequest createNamedQueryRequest = new CreateNamedQueryRequest()
22               .withDatabase(ExampleConstants.ATHENA_DEFAULT_DATABASE)
```

```
23              .withQueryString(ExampleConstants.ATHENA_SAMPLE_QUERY)
24              .withDescription("Sample Description")
25              .withName("SampleQuery");
26
27      // Call Athena to create the named query. If it fails, an exception is thrown.
28      CreateNamedQueryResult createNamedQueryResult = client.createNamedQuery(
            createNamedQueryRequest);
29  }
30 }
```

Delete a Named Query

```
1 package com.amazonaws.services.athena.sdksamples;
2
3 import com.amazonaws.services.athena.AmazonAthena;
4 import com.amazonaws.services.athena.model.CreateNamedQueryRequest;
5 import com.amazonaws.services.athena.model.CreateNamedQueryResult;
6 import com.amazonaws.services.athena.model.DeleteNamedQueryRequest;
7 import com.amazonaws.services.athena.model.DeleteNamedQueryResult;
8
9 /**
10 * DeleteNamedQueryExample
11 * ------------------------------------
12 * This code shows how to delete a named query by using the named query ID.
13 */
14 public class DeleteNamedQueryExample
15 {
16     private static String getNamedQueryId(AmazonAthena athenaClient)
17     {
18         // Create the NameQuery Request.
19         CreateNamedQueryRequest createNamedQueryRequest = new CreateNamedQueryRequest()
20                 .withDatabase(ExampleConstants.ATHENA_DEFAULT_DATABASE)
21                 .withQueryString(ExampleConstants.ATHENA_SAMPLE_QUERY)
22                 .withName("SampleQueryName")
23                 .withDescription("Sample Description");
24
25         // Create the named query. If it fails, an exception is thrown.
26         CreateNamedQueryResult createNamedQueryResult = athenaClient.createNamedQuery(
                createNamedQueryRequest);
27         return createNamedQueryResult.getNamedQueryId();
28     }
29
30     public static void main(String[] args) throws Exception
31     {
32         // Build an Athena client
33         AthenaClientFactory factory = new AthenaClientFactory();
34         AmazonAthena client = factory.createClient();
35
36         String sampleNamedQueryId = getNamedQueryId(client);
37
38         // Create the delete named query request
39         DeleteNamedQueryRequest deleteNamedQueryRequest = new DeleteNamedQueryRequest()
40                 .withNamedQueryId(sampleNamedQueryId);
41
```

```
42          // Delete the named query
43          DeleteNamedQueryResult deleteNamedQueryResult = client.deleteNamedQuery(
                deleteNamedQueryRequest);
44      }
45 }
```

List Named Queries

```
1 package com.amazonaws.services.athena.sdksamples;
2
3 import com.amazonaws.services.athena.AmazonAthena;
4 import com.amazonaws.services.athena.model.ListNamedQueriesRequest;
5 import com.amazonaws.services.athena.model.ListNamedQueriesResult;
6
7 import java.util.List;
8
9 /**
10 * ListNamedQueryExample
11 * -------------------------------------
12 * This code shows how to obtain a list of named query IDs.
13 */
14 public class ListNamedQueryExample
15 {
16     public static void main(String[] args) throws Exception
17     {
18         // Build an Athena client
19         AthenaClientFactory factory = new AthenaClientFactory();
20         AmazonAthena client = factory.createClient();
21
22         // Build the request
23         ListNamedQueriesRequest listNamedQueriesRequest = new ListNamedQueriesRequest();
24
25         // Get the list results.
26         ListNamedQueriesResult listNamedQueriesResult = client.listNamedQueries(
                listNamedQueriesRequest);
27
28         // Process the results.
29         boolean hasMoreResults = true;
30
31         while (hasMoreResults) {
32             List<String> namedQueryIds = listNamedQueriesResult.getNamedQueryIds();
33             // process named query IDs
34
35             // If nextToken is not null, there are more results. Get the next page of results.
36             if (listNamedQueriesResult.getNextToken() != null) {
37                 listNamedQueriesResult = client.listNamedQueries(
38                         listNamedQueriesRequest.withNextToken(listNamedQueriesResult.
                            getNextToken()));
39             }
40             else {
41                 hasMoreResults = false;
42             }
43         }
44     }
```

Using the Previous Version of the JDBC Driver

We recommend that you use the current version of the driver. However, if you need to use the previous version, follow the steps in this section to download and configure the driver.

Download the Previous Version of the JDBC Driver

1. Download the driver (JDBC 4.1 and Java 8 compatible) from this location in Amazon S3 https://s3. amazonaws.com/athena-downloads/drivers/JDBC/AthenaJDBC_1.1.0/AthenaJDBC41-1.1.0.jar.

2. Download the license: https://s3.amazonaws.com/athena-downloads/drivers/JDBC/AthenaJDBC_1.1.0/ docs/LICENSE.txt, and the third-party licenses: https://s3.amazonaws.com/athena-downloads/drivers/ JDBC/AthenaJDBC_1.1.0/docs/third-party-licenses.txt.

3. Use the AWS CLI with the following command:

```
1 aws s3 cp s3://athena-downloads/drivers/JDBC/AthenaJDBC_1.1.0/AthenaJDBC41-1.1.0.jar [
    local_directory]
```

Specify the Connection String

To specify the JDBC driver connection URL in your custom application, use the string in this format:

```
1 jdbc:awsathena://athena.{REGION}.amazonaws.com:443
```

where {REGION} is a region identifier, such as us-west-2. For information on Athena regions see Regions.

Specify the JDBC Driver Class Name

To use the driver in custom applications, set up your Java class path to the location of the JAR file that you downloaded from Amazon S3 https://s3.amazonaws.com/athena-downloads/drivers/JDBC/AthenaJDBC_1.1. 0/AthenaJDBC41-1.1.0.jar in the previous section. This makes the classes within the JAR available for use. The main JDBC driver class is com.amazonaws.athena.jdbc.AthenaDriver.

Provide the JDBC Driver Credentials

To gain access to AWS services and resources, such as Athena and the Amazon S3 buckets, provide JDBC driver credentials to your application.

To provide credentials in the Java code for your application:

1. Use a class which implements the http://docs.aws.amazon.com/AWSJavaSDK/latest/javadoc/com/ amazonaws/auth/AWSCredentialsProvider.html.

2. Set the JDBC property, aws_credentials_provider_class, equal to the class name, and include it in your classpath.

3. To include constructor parameters, set the JDBC property aws_credentials_provider_arguments as specified in the following section about configuration options.

Another method to supply credentials to BI tools, such as SQL Workbench, is to supply the credentials used for the JDBC as AWS access key and AWS secret key for the JDBC properties for user and password, respectively.

Users who connect through the JDBC driver and have custom access policies attached to their profiles need permissions for policy actions in addition to those in the Amazon Athena API Reference.

Policies

You must allow JDBC users to perform a set of policy-specific actions. These actions are not part of the Athena API. If the following actions are not allowed, users will be unable to see databases and tables:

- `athena:GetCatalogs`
- `athena:GetExecutionEngine`
- `athena:GetExecutionEngines`
- `athena:GetNamespace`
- `athena:GetNamespaces`
- `athena:GetTable`
- `athena:GetTables`

Configure the JDBC Driver Options

You can configure the following options for the deprecated version of the JDBC driver. With this version of the driver, you can also pass parameters using the standard JDBC URL syntax, for example: `jdbc:awsathena://athena.us-west-1.amazonaws.com:443?max_error_retries=20&connection_timeout=20000`.

Options for the Previous Version of JDBC Driver

Property Name	Description	Default Value	Is Required
s3_staging_dir	The S3 location to which your query output is written, for example s3://query-results-bucket/folder/, which is established under Settings in the Athena Console, https://console.aws.amazon.com/athena/. The JDBC driver then asks Athena to read the results and provide rows of data back to the user.	N/A	Yes
query_results_encryption_option	The encryption method to use for the directory specified by s3_staging_dir. If not specified, the location is not encrypted. Valid values are SSE_S3, SSE_KMS, and CSE_KMS.	N/A	No

Property Name	Description	Default Value	Is Required
query_results_aws_kms_key	The Key ID of the AWS customer master key (CMK) to use if query_results_encry specifies SSE-KMS or CSE-KMS. For example, 123abcde-4e56-56f7 -g890-1234h5678i9j .	N/A	No
aws_credentials_provider_class	The credentials provider class name, which implements the AWSCredentialsProvider interface.	N/A	No
aws_credentials_provider_arguments	Arguments for the credentials provider constructor as comma-separated values.	N/A	No
max_error_retries	The maximum number of retries that the JDBC client attempts to make a request to Athena.	10	No
connection_timeout	The maximum amount of time, in milliseconds, to make a successful connection to Athena before an attempt is terminated.	10,000	No
socket_timeout	The maximum amount of time, in milliseconds, to wait for a socket in order to send data to Athena.	10,000	No
retry_base_delay	Minimum delay amount, in milliseconds, between retrying attempts to connect Athena.	100	No
retry_max_backoff_time	Maximum delay amount, in milliseconds, between retrying attempts to connect to Athena.	1000	No
log_path	Local path of the Athena JDBC driver logs. If no log path is provided, then no log files are created.	N/A	No

Property Name	Description	Default Value	Is Required
log_level	Log level of the Athena JDBC driver logs. Valid values: INFO, DEBUG, WARN, ERROR, ALL, OFF, FATAL, TRACE.	N/A	No

Examples: Using the Previous Version of the JDBC Driver with the JDK

The following code examples demonstrate how to use the previous version of the JDBC driver in a Java application. These examples assume that the AWS JAVA SDK is included in your classpath, specifically the `aws-java-sdk-core` module, which includes the authorization packages (`com.amazonaws.auth.*`) referenced in the examples.

Example Example: Creating a Driver

```
1    Properties info = new Properties();
2    info.put("user", "AWSAccessKey");
3    info.put("password", "AWSSecretAccessKey");
4    info.put("s3_staging_dir", "s3://S3 Bucket Location/");
5    info.put("aws_credentials_provider_class","com.amazonaws.auth.
         DefaultAWSCredentialsProviderChain");
6
7    Class.forName("com.amazonaws.athena.jdbc.AthenaDriver");
8
9    Connection connection = DriverManager.getConnection("jdbc:awsathena://athena.us-east-1.
         amazonaws.com:443/", info);
```

The following examples demonstrate different ways to use a credentials provider that implements the `AWSCredentialsProvider` interface with the previous version of the JDBC driver.

Example Example: Using a Credentials Provider

```
1 Properties myProps = new Properties();
2        myProps.put("aws_credentials_provider_class","com.amazonaws.auth.
             PropertiesFileCredentialsProvider");
3        myProps.put("aws_credentials_provider_arguments","/Users/myUser/.athenaCredentials");
```

In this case, the file `/Users/myUser/.athenaCredentials` should contain the following:

```
1 accessKey = ACCESSKEY
2 secretKey = SECRETKEY
```

Replace the right part of the assignments with your account's AWS access and secret keys.

Example Example: Using a Credentials Provider with Multiple Arguments
This example shows an example credentials provider, `CustomSessionsCredentialsProvider`, that uses an access and secret key in addition to a session token. `CustomSessionsCredentialsProvider` is shown for example only and is not included in the driver. The signature of the class looks like the following:

```
1 public CustomSessionsCredentialsProvider(String accessId, String secretKey, String token)
2        {
3        //...
4        }
```

You would then set the properties as follows:

```
1 Properties myProps = new Properties();
2         myProps.put("aws_credentials_provider_class","com.amazonaws.athena.jdbc.
              CustomSessionsCredentialsProvider");
3         String providerArgs = "My_Access_Key," + "My_Secret_Key," + "My_Token";
4         myProps.put("aws_credentials_provider_arguments",providerArgs);
```

If you use the http://docs.aws.amazon.com/AWSJavaSDK/latest/javadoc/com/amazonaws/auth/ InstanceProfileCredentialsProvider.html, you don't need to supply any credential provider arguments because they are provided using the Amazon EC2 instance profile for the instance on which you are running your application. You would still set the `aws_credentials_provider_class` property to this class name, however.

Policies for the JDBC Driver Earlier than Version 1.1.0

Use these deprecated actions in policies **only** with JDBC drivers **earlier than version 1.1.0**. If you are upgrading the JDBC driver, replace policy statements that allow or deny deprecated actions with the appropriate API actions as listed or errors will occur.

Deprecated Policy-Specific Action	Corresponding Athena API Action
athena:RunQuery	athena:StartQueryExecution
athena:CancelQueryExecution	athena:StopQueryExecution
athena:GetQueryExecutions	athena:ListQueryExecutions

Service Limits

Note
You can contact AWS Support to request a limit increase for the limits listed here.

- By default, concurrency limits on your account allow you to submit twenty concurrent DDL queries (used for creating tables and adding partitions) and twenty concurrent SELECT queries at a time. This is a soft limit and you can request a limit increase for concurrent queries.

  Concurrency limits in Athena are defined as the number of queries that can be submitted to the service concurrently. You can submit up to twenty queries of the same type (DDL or SELECT) at a time. If you submit a query that exceeds the concurrent query limit, the Athena API displays an error message: "You have exceeded the limit for the number of queries you can run concurrently. Reduce the number of concurrent queries submitted by this account. Contact customer support to request a concurrent query limit increase."

  After you submit your queries to Athena, it processes the queries by assigning resources based on the overall service load and the amount of incoming requests. We continuously monitor and make adjustments to the service so that your queries process as fast as possible.

- If you use Athena in regions where AWS Glue is available, migrate to AWS Glue Catalog. See Upgrading to the AWS Glue Data Catalog Step-by-Step. If you have migrated to AWS Glue, for service limits on tables, databases, and partitions in Athena, see AWS Glue Limits.

- If you have not migrated to AWS Glue Catalog, you can request a limit increase.

- You may encounter a limit for Amazon S3 buckets per account, which is 100. Athena also needs a separate bucket to log results.

- Query timeout: 30 minutes.

Document History

This documentation is associated with the May, 18, 2017 version of Amazon Athena.

Latest documentation update: June 5, 2018.

Change	Description	Release Date
Added support for views. Added guidelines for schema manipulations for various data storage formats.	Added support for views. For information, see Views. Updated this guide with guidance on handling schema updates for various data storage formats. For information, see Handling Schema Updates.	June 5, 2018
Increased default query concurrency limits from five to twenty.	You can submit and run up to twenty DDL queries and twenty SELECT queries at a time. For information, see Service Limits.	May 17, 2018
Added query tabs, and an ability to configure auto-complete in the Query Editor.	Added query tabs, and an ability to configure auto-complete in the Query Editor. For information, see Using the Console.	May 8, 2018
Released the JDBC driver version 2.0.2.	Released the new version of the JDBC driver (version 2.0.2). For information, see Using Athena with the JDBC Driver.	April 19, 2018
Added auto-complete for typing queries in the Athena console.	Added auto-complete for typing queries in the Athena console.	April 6, 2018
Added an ability to create Athena tables for CloudTrail log files directly from the CloudTrail console.	Added an ability to automatically create Athena tables for CloudTrail log files directly from the CloudTrail console. For information, see Creating a Table for CloudTrail Logs in the CloudTrail Console.	March 15, 2018
Added support for securely offloading intermediate data to disk for queries with GROUP BY.	Added an ability to securely offload intermediate data to disk for memory-intensive queries that use the GROUP BY clause. This improves the reliability of such queries, preventing "Query resource exhausted" errors. For more information, see the release note for February 2, 2018.	February 2, 2018
Added support for Presto version 0.172.	Upgraded the underlying engine in Amazon Athena to a version based on Presto version 0.172. For more information, see the release note for January 19, 2018.	January 19, 2018

Change	Description	Release Date
Added support for the ODBC Driver.	Added support for connecting Athena to the ODBC Driver. For information, see Connecting to Amazon Athena with ODBC.	November 13, 2017
Added support for Asia Pacific (Seoul), Asia Pacific (Mumbai), and EU (London) regions. Added support for querying geospatial data.	Added support for querying geospatial data, and for Asia Pacific (Seoul), Asia Pacific (Mumbai), EU (London) regions. For information, see Querying Geospatial Data and AWS Regions and Endpoints.	November 1, 2017
Added support for EU (Frankfurt).	Added support for EU (Frankfurt). For a list of supported regions, see AWS Regions and Endpoints.	October 19, 2017
Added support for named Athena queries with AWS CloudFormation.	Added support for creating named Athena queries with AWS CloudFormation. For more information, see AWS::Athena::NamedQuery in the AWS CloudFormation User Guide.	October 3, 2017
Added support for Asia Pacific (Sydney).	Added support for Asia Pacific (Sydney). For a list of supported regions, see AWS Regions and Endpoints.	September 25, 2017
Added a section to this guide for querying AWS Service logs and different types of data, including maps, arrays, nested data, and data containing JSON.	Added examples for Querying AWS Service Logs and for querying different types of data in Athena. For information, see Querying Data in Amazon Athena Tables.	September 5, 2017
Added support for AWS Glue Data Catalog.	Added integration with the AWS Glue Data Catalog and a migration wizard for updating from the Athena managed data catalog to the AWS Glue Data Catalog. For more information, see Integration with AWS Glue and AWS Glue.	August 14, 2017
Added support for Grok SerDe.	Added support for Grok SerDe, which provides easier pattern matching for records in unstructured text files such as logs. For more information, see Grok SerDe. Added keyboard shortcuts to scroll through query history using the console (CTRL + / using Windows, CMD + / using Mac).	August 4, 2017

Change	Description	Release Date
Added support for Asia Pacific (Tokyo).	Added support for Asia Pacific (Tokyo) and Asia Pacific (Singapore). For a list of supported regions, see AWS Regions and Endpoints.	June 22, 2017
Added support for EU (Ireland).	Added support for EU (Ireland). For more information, see AWS Regions and Endpoints.	June 8, 2017
Added an Amazon Athena API and AWS CLI support.	Added an Amazon Athena API and AWS CLI support for Athena. Updated JDBC driver to version 1.1.0.	May 19, 2017
Added support for Amazon S3 data encryption.	Added support for Amazon S3 data encryption and released a JDBC driver update (version 1.0.1) with encryption support, improvements, and bug fixes. For more information, see Configuring Encryption Options.	April 4, 2017
Added the AWS CloudTrail SerDe.	Added the AWS CloudTrail SerDe, improved performance, fixed partition issues. For more information, see CloudTrail SerDe.[See the AWS documentation website for more details]	March 24, 2017
Added support for US East (Ohio).	Added support for Avro SerDe and OpenCSVSerDe for Processing CSV, US East (Ohio), and bulk editing columns in the console wizard. Improved performance on large Parquet tables.	February 20, 2017
	The initial release of the Amazon Athena User Guide.	November, 2016

AWS Glossary

For the latest AWS terminology, see the AWS Glossary in the *AWS General Reference*.

www.ingramcontent.com/pod-product-compliance
Lightning Source LLC
LaVergne TN
LVHW082037050326
832904LV00005B/221